Developing Your Company Culture

Developing Your Company Culture

The Joy of Leadership

A HANDBOOK FOR LEADERS AND MANAGERS

Barry Phegan, Ph.D.

CONTEXT
PRESS

Developing Your Company Culture

The Joy of Leadership—A Handbook for Leaders and Managers

Copyright © 1996 by Barry Phegan
Third printing 2000

Context Press
Meridian Group, Inc.
1827 A Fifth Street
Berkeley, CA 94710
Phone   1-800-363-7434
        1-510-848-4258
Fax   1-510-848-4257
Email   dialogue@meridiangrp.net
Web   http://www.meridiangrp.net

Book Design: Richard Yee
Illustrations: Warren Douglas and Hugh White
Production: Canterbury Press, Berkeley, California
Printing: Central Plains Book Manufacturing, Winfield, Kansas

Library of Congress Catalog Card Number: 94-92384
ISBN 0-9642205-0-4 $12.95
Manufactured in the United States of America

Contents

Dedicated to cultural leaders—
who build engaging, productive
work places.

ACKNOWLEDGMENTS

I could not have written this handbook without many years of discussions with my ally, mentor, and close friend Royal Foote. His thoughtful and humane guidance largely shaped Meridian Group's practice. Royal's deep interest in the theory and practice of social change has made it possible for me, all of us in Meridian Group, and our clients to experience finer and more productive lives, at work and elsewhere. Parts of this book come from theories developed by Royal that will be more fully presented in his forthcoming book on the humanization of work.

I want to thank the many managers in our client companies, who have walked arm in arm with us over the last 20 years doing a very hard thing—developing humane, open, and engaging organizational cultures.

Thanks also to my family, partners, friends, and associates who shaped my life and reviewed drafts of this book. Thank you, Al, Bill, Bob, Britt, Chris, Dave, Diane, Dick, Dinah, Donna, Fred, Greg, Jack, James, Jamie, Janet, Janice, Jim, Jocelyn, John, Kathryn, Kay, Lenny, Linda, Liz, Mike, Pat, Paul, Peter, Richard, Robert, Roger, Sam, Sharon, Steve, Terry, Tom, Tracy, Verona, Warren, West, and to Warren Douglas and Hugh White for illustrations, Dave Weinstein, Jean Schiffman, and Pat Shell for editing, and Richard Yee for book design. The book is what it is because of you.

Shortcomings, errors, and omissions I claim as mine.

The purpose of a dance is not to go from one corner of the room to the other in the shortest possible time. It is to enjoy the getting there. We are given one chance on this earth. We should live well and live right, at work and at home.

As one production line worker said, three years into the work culture change effort, "I didn't used to talk about what I do at work, at home. Now I talk about it all the time." She had put together parts of her life that too many people keep separate.

Improving the quality of people's work lives makes this hard work of culture change worthwhile.

Introduction

PEOPLE ENGAGED WITH THEIR TASK

Typically, efforts to develop a work culture begin with support from the top. In a major U.S. corporation, a vice president urged Bob, a unit manager in Texas, to try something new at his facility. I invited Bob to visit a plant in Northern California that over several years had developed a mature work culture. Bob was given the tour by Gerry, the plant manager.

As we approached one production area, an operator left the line to greet us. Gerry introduced Bob to the operator who, with a friendly smile and handshake, asked Bob why was he visiting.

The operator briefly described his production area, and then said, "This is a sanitary cap area. Please use mine. You can give it to Gerry when you leave. I'll get another from my supervisor." The operator continued talking with Bob for a few minutes and then he looked at his watch. "Gosh, we've been talking longer than I thought. Please excuse me. I have to get back. I had asked my supervisor to watch the line while I came over. It's been nice talking. Enjoy your tour." He shook hands and walked away.

Bob was amazed. Here was a union operator asking his supervisor to relieve him, initiating a conversation with a visitor accompanied by a manager five levels above him, conscious of sanitation—and indirectly, gently scolding Gerry about caps. The operator did this in a friendly, open manner. Later Bob said, "I knew then this was the type of atmosphere I wanted in my plant."

Work in any organization should be engaging and deeply satisfying. It should mirror a good life. As the year 2000 approaches, some American companies are learning to create open and humane organizational cultures that engage employees, allowing them to fulfill themselves at work as they do at home.

This is something new in the world. It is distinctly American, and only a handful of companies have gone very far with it, but it is definitely the direction where all U.S. companies will move. Four examples:

▶ At a continuous process plant, the new manager's assignment was "Turn it around or shut it down." He suspected the productivity and safety problems were not issues of skill or training but culture. After two years the management team moved from mistrust and defensiveness to a powerful sense of teamwork and mastery. This was accomplished by following actions like those outlined in this book. Employees responded with more openness and involvement. Productivity rose while costs dropped dramatically. When the opportunity arose to acquire control of a major regional competitor, the management team quickly integrated the two operations, securing everyone's future. None of this would have been possible under the original work culture of the plant.

▶ This 800-person food-processing operation is one of several in the corporation. After three years of work to develop the culture using the principles outlined in this book, productivity made one of those sudden, predictable, evolutionary jumps—it rose 40% over a three-month period. The plant manager commented that the consulting cost for one year was less than the cost of one day of can lids.

▶ In a transportation and warehousing company, after developing their work culture for three years using the principles in this book, the management team became more open to change. Supervisors responded by involving first line employees in decisions. Work-related injuries and grievances dropped while productivity increased steadily as relationships with the union improved. As union contract negotiation time approached, both union leaders and unit managers agreed that their improved relationships averted an almost certain strike. In a win-win work culture, everybody succeeds.

▶ After four years of developing his unit's culture with the methods suggested here, a manager sketched a new organization chart, describing the current state of his unit and how things actually worked. He drew no lines. He placed himself at the bottom and nonmanagement employees on top. In between were groups of people in functional areas without titles, grouped as support to nonmanagers. This unit, just one of many in a large company, was successful in almost every way, becoming a trailblazer that others followed.

Organizations like these are moving to the front, responding rapidly to shifting markets and technologies, attracting and holding the right people, and becoming sensitive and responsive to their customers. Their products are top-quality and low-cost. These companies have high productivity, safety, employee satisfaction, and resilience.

As Jack Welch, Chairman and CEO of General Electric Company said at a recent speech* "We now know where productivity—real and limitless productivity—comes from. It comes from challenged, empowered, excited, rewarded teams of people. It comes from engaging every single mind in the organization...making everyone part of the action and allowing everyone to have a voice—a role—in the success of the enterprise. The paradox is that these brutally competitive times will be the most exciting, rewarding, and fulfilling of all for those fortunate enough to be part of [such] companies."

To a visitor, these companies may look relaxed, even casual. Managers rarely give orders—though they give a lot of information and help—and rarely appear to make decisions, though they strongly guide and shape decision-making processes. Employees at all levels experience trust and psychological safety. Rank, authority, and control issues do not dominate their landscapes. These companies see diversity of the work force as one reason for their success.

By reducing top-down control and opening the system to self-control, humane corporate cultures focus the power of people on their task. These developed companies, like a mature person, determine their own future and experience few limits.

Developing an engaging organizational culture is not as complicated as rocket science. While it is hard to do, it can be deeply satisfying for you, your people, and your stockholders.

---

*Excerpted with permission from a speech presented at the Economic Club of Detroit, Michigan, May 16, 1994.

HIGHLIGHTS OF THE BOOK

► **Culture sets the stage for success.** It is your organization's culture that leads to success or to failure, page 6.

► **Leaders can manage their organization's culture** as straight-forwardly as they manage production, page 15.

► **Look in the mirror.** What people do reflects the work culture and what leaders do. Leaders must be role models, page 7.

► **Reading your organization's cultural themes.** Learn the forces that guide your organization, page 63. A key is—

► **The interview,** which builds closer relationships, trust, and understanding with the people in your organization, page 58.

► **Cultural development is evolutionary.** Evolution is not a mystery—it is understandable and manageable, page 45.

► **High productivity is easy.** By developing the work culture, you will have a highly productive organization, page 17.

► **Satisfaction and productivity go hand in hand.** They are com-plementary, page 131.

► **Leading the decision process.** How you make decisions is a key to engaging your people, page 73.

► **The "Parallel Organization."** Creating an organizational structure to rapidly develop the work culture, page 64.

► **Authoritarianism is the limit of productivity.** Certain personalities limit your organization's productivity, page 29.

► **Training dollars are mostly wasted.** Training does not get at the issues. People know what to do. You must get rid of what is blocking them from doing it, page 17.

► **Developing the work culture has great leverage.** There is no more profitable way to spend your time, page 4.

A HANDBOOK FOR LEADERS AND MANAGERS

I wrote this as a handbook for corporate leaders and managers who sense that success comes hand in hand with developing an engaging, open, and humane organizational culture but want guidance in getting there.

Companies usually pilot their culture development effort at a willing unit or plant, with strong support from the president or a vice president. This is how it should be. Cultural evolution always begins where there is a readiness. After one or two years, success speaks for itself. Then others join.

All situations described in this book are from U.S. companies I have worked with over the last 20 years—only the names are changed. While these companies are mostly manufacturing, retailing, health services, and transportation and distribution, the lessons apply equally to any function in any productive organization.

It is almost impossible to see a culture objectively if you are inside it. This book describes how to use an outside guide on the journey.

Good luck to all of you who seek a better workplace for yourself, and your colleagues. It takes courage to explore and lead the company culture. Even with your management team alongside, it can be a hard and sometimes lonesome trail. But it is always rewarding.

HOW TO READ THIS BOOK

Do not expect to read this handbook from cover to cover as an unbroken chain of analytic reasoning or as a stream of continuous actions. It is not a novel, story, or parable. It is a collection of tested principles and tools for developing an open, humane, engaging, and therefore productive company culture.

If you have not yet taken steps to develop your organization's culture, you might find parts of this guidebook obscure. Managers who have developed their company cultures often have difficulty communicating the process to others. Their results are visible, but language and analysis are inadequate vehicles for fully conveying the experience of doing it. This book has the same limitations.

There is no one path through any organization's cultural landscape and certainly no one way to build an open, humane, and engaging company culture. There are as many paths as there are work cultures and as many paths in those cultures as there are people. We must make our own way in this world. Please make your own way through this handbook's three sections.

Section 1—The stage. Some elements, definitions, and principles of organizational culture and culture change—personality, group dynamics, systems theory, and evolution. If you find this first section heavy going, please jump to Section 2.

Section 2—Just do it. The principles in practice. Hands on examples of what managers do to develop their corporate culture.

Section 3—Reflections. Thoughts from two decades of working with managers on developing their organization's cultures— what is an arrested work culture? What is an ideal work culture? Where are U.S. companies headed?

☞ Marks practical suggestions—how you might put the material to work in your organization.

ABOUT THE AUTHOR

For 20 years, I have helped companies build organizational cultures that are open to what members can contribute. For twenty years before that, I was an employee, manager, and owner in companies in Australia, Sweden, Canada, and the U.S.

Marriage, raising children, working in organizations large and small, owning businesses, being a manager, and teaching, all contribute to my understanding and commitment to my work. These experiences set the stage for what is in this book.

I wrote this handbook during an intense few months. Some pages were written as separate pieces over the last 20 years for courses at the University of California and occasionally for client seminars.

As I pulled these pieces together, rewrote them, and added new thoughts, I saw the book as a landscape of an open work culture, a rich and varied terrain of mountains and plains, of light and shadow, partly visible, partly obscured, partly foreground, but mostly distant and not yet explored.

Barry Phegan
Berkeley, California

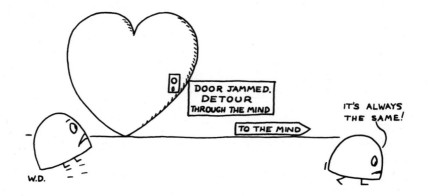

The Stage

There is nothing more practical than a good theory. –K. Lewin

You would not build a bridge without understanding structural mechanics. You would not perform a heart transplant without practice. But with neither theory nor practice, managers often tackle something much more difficult—their organization's culture. That's why successful culture change is rare.

This section describes the principles needed to create an engaging organizational culture. These principles, developed during 20 years working with companies large and small, are not exactly a prescription, but they work.

Chapter 1—Organizational culture and leadership. A culture is a field of influences that set the stage for what everyone does; we will look at the nature of company culture.

Chapter 2—The development of culture. A culture's development is almost the same as a person's development. Leadership's behavior determines how far and how fast the organization's culture will develop; we will explore personality theory, developmental theory, authority, and control.

Chapter 3—Groups and systems. Organizations are large groups with certain ways of their own; we will look at group dynamics. Organizations are whole integrated systems, not independent departments or events; we will look at general systems theory.

Chapter 4—Evolution and culture. Work cultures change by evolving and leadership shapes that evolution. Evolution follows an understandable and predictable path; we will examine the steps and process of evolution.

section one

1

Organizational Culture and Leadership

Culture is what people do and what their actions mean to them. Culture is the ideas, interests, values and attitudes shared by a group. It is the backgrounds, skills, traditions, communication and decision processes, myths, fears, hopes, aspirations, and expectations experienced by you and your people. Your organization's culture is how people feel about doing a good job and what makes equipment and people work together in harmony. It is the glue that holds, the oil that lubricates. It is history expressed in the present.

Your organization's culture is the intricate pattern of how people do things, what they believe in, what is rewarded and penalized. It is how and why people take different jobs in the company. It is how parts of the company view other parts and how each department behaves as a result of those views. It shows up in jokes and cartoons pinned on bulletin boards—or kept in the desk drawer and shown only to the "in" group. It is what everybody knows—except, perhaps, the boss.

Newcomers take up the organization's culture. We transmit culture through dress, style, and language, by what we say—and do not say—and what we do—and do not do.

Corporate cultures are as distinctive as fingerprints. People at Hewlett-Packard have a strong sense of what someone means by "It's the H-P way." People at Bank of America know what is meant when someone says, "We don't do that at B of A."

AN ORGANIZATION'S CULTURE IS LIKE A MAGNETIC FIELD

Imagine trying to line up thousands of iron filings sprinkled on a page—without a magnet. How long would that take? Now take a magnet to the page—they align instantly. A culture is like a magnetic field; it influences and aligns everything in it. Nothing escapes.

We are influenced by cultural fields: a trusting atmosphere, a safe place to speak, a supportive environment.

Changing the organization's cultural field may be hard to do, but it is simple to understand. When you change the field, you change everyone and everything in it. Working on the human side of work culture is one of the most efficient actions a company can take.

❖ **The cultural field aligns everyone and everything.**
❖ **Developing your work culture has very high leverage.**

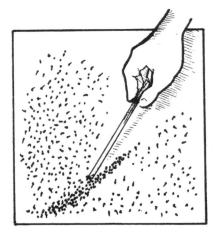 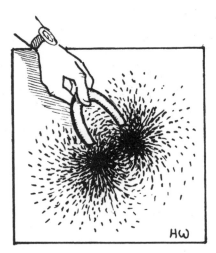

WE RESPOND TO OUR ENVIRONMENT

It is context that gives events meaning. –unknown

What we do depends on two things—our personality and the situation. As we move from situation to situation, we change our behavior as appropriate. In a classroom, we sit quietly. In a ball game, we shout and run. We have not changed—the situation has.

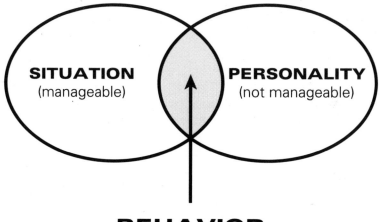

SITUATION
(manageable)

PERSONALITY
(not manageable)

BEHAVIOR

As a leader, you can do very little about someone's personality (and you should not attempt to), but you can do a lot about the situation. The situation, or culture, is all you can really affect. If you develop an engaging work culture, everyone will see that engagement is appropriate; they will then bring more of themselves to work.

❖   **It is the situation that tells us what to do.**
❖   **It is largely the situation that explains what we have done.**
❖   **If you want to understand an event, look first at the situation.**
❖   **If you want to change behavior, change the situation.**

CULTURE IS THE STAGE FOR ACTIONS

"All the world's a stage, and all the men and women merely players." –W. Shakespeare, *As You Like It*

A Berkeley Repertory Theatre actor once told me that actors do not invent a character, they simply leave in the wings all the unwanted aspects of their personality palette. Only necessary parts are allowed on stage.

As healthy working people, we have access to a wide range of personality traits and behaviors. In everyday life, we show a limited part of this spectrum. Given the right stage, we can surprise even our close friends as we become perhaps a clown, perhaps Hamlet.

How we choose to act depends largely on the situation, the stage. Culture is our stage, exaggerating some traits, inhibiting others. You see this both with countries and with corporations. Tidy Swiss, formal British, easygoing Texan, innovative Californian, button-down IBM executive, casual Microsoft employee, analytic H-P engineer. These people are the same as you and I except for their national and company cultures. Their culture makes the difference—and what a difference that is.

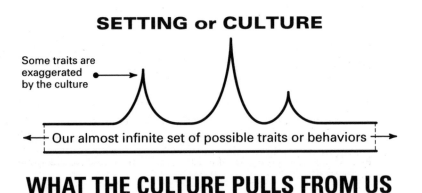

SETTING or CULTURE

Some traits are exaggerated by the culture

Our almost infinite set of possible traits or behaviors

WHAT THE CULTURE PULLS FROM US

BEHAVIOR IS A MIRROR OF CULTURE AND LEADERSHIP

*"[Culture] is a product of man: he projects himself into it, he recognizes himself in it, that critical mirror alone offers him his image." —*J.P. Sartre, *The Words*

What people do in an organization reflects the organization's culture, the stage on which they play. Leaders set that stage. So what people do on that stage tells us about their leaders.

"What you do speaks so loudly, I can't hear what you say." Actions speak loudly. If leaders behave in caring ways, so will others. If they behave aggressively, so will others. Leaders who want cooperation and involvement will get it if they show it in their daily actions. If they do not show it they will not get it.

You can use this mirror of others' behavior to understand what you and your managers should do differently. If you think employees are not behaving properly, perhaps you are giving the wrong signals.

As you change, the stage will change and so will others' behavior. For feedback on your leadership look at what people actually do—not at what they "should" do—and at how they feel about their work.

☞ To understand your organization's culture and how you influence it, talk with your people, getting to know them better, understanding their work experiences, learning what they do and what their work means to them. A simple way to do this is with the "interview," (page 58), which can profoundly affect how your work culture develops.

❖ **People act according to the situation. What people do gives you information about the leadership.**

❖ **Leaders set the stage. Leaders can change that stage.**

MOST OF US FOLLOW THE LEADER

Most of us are flexible, accepting our organization's culture more or less as it is, going along without much complaint. We are adaptable. If the work culture is friendly, we will be friendly; if the work culture is critical, we will be critical.

People's potential behavior is widely distributed over any personality characteristic. Take "openness" to others. At one end are the 10% who will be open no matter what their work culture is like. At the other end of the spectrum are people who are closed, no matter what the situation. The flexible 80% in the middle accept whichever side is most influential at the moment. Most people have the potential to be open but hold back unless they are encouraged. Most people want to feel good about their work, be productive, have satisfying relationships. This is why you can develop the work culture—because most people want it.

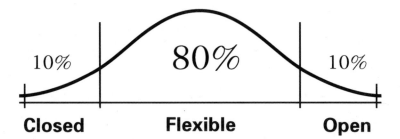

10%	80%	10%
Closed	**Flexible**	**Open**

Many underdeveloped work cultures are strongly influenced by a closed, fighting minority. The flexible middle responds by being closed and adversarial, not because they want to but because they sense that is expected. If leaders behave in positive ways, the flexible middle will follow.

As a company's culture develops, this flexible middle moves quickly, sometimes surprisingly so. "Why didn't they do this before?" The answer: "Because until now they did not know it was wanted or permissible."

❖ **You can rely on most people to rise to the occasion.**
❖ **The flexible middle is your greatest ally.**

ROOTS OF WESTERN CULTURE—
SCYLLA AND CHARYBDIS

Three thousand years ago, as our Greek ancestors emerged from their misty, preconscious "Dreamtime," they told of fabulous journeys taken by Odysseus and Jason. These mythical heroes each sailed through the dangerous Straits of Messina that separate Sicily from Italy. Two monsters guarded the straits, enticing unwary travelers to their death.

Scylla, a once-beautiful nymph transformed by a jealous goddess, lived on the rocky Italian side. She seized and devoured sailors. Charybdis stole Hercules' cattle. Hercules hurled her into the sea across the straits from Scylla. There she created a whirlpool, pulling unwary travelers to their doom.

These two edges, rocks and whirlpool, symbolize an early division of our mind, splitting the seamless, at-one-with-nature experience of primitive people. This split represents extremes, dangers we face if we do not navigate a balanced course. Success in life means navigating a safe passage between these two sides of our personality, and of our organization's culture. Each calls us seductively to its shore. These extremes have many names:

SCYLLA	CHARYBDIS
Rocks	Whirlpool
Hard	Soft
Masculine	Feminine
Rigid	Flexible
Action	Meaning
Structure	Process
Closed	Open
Task	People
Body	Mind
Yang	Yin
Earth	Heaven
Operations	Human
Bottom	Top
Infrastructure	Superstructure

After Greek and Roman times, Western culture separated formalized religion from the state—"Render therefore unto Caesar the things which are Caesar's; and unto God the things that are God's" (The Holy Bible; Matthew; 22:21.) In doing this, we recognized our recently evolved self-awareness. Now we were conscious of an external world and an internal self.

Fifteen hundred years later, after Galileo's persecution, Western culture separated a third item—science. Sir Isaac Newton and others defined the ground rules of science, a platform for our present world view. Some argue that today's science and technology, emphasizing analytic thinking, often undermine rather than support humanness.

For several hundred years, science has dominated American organizations. We coursed fast and close to those craggy shores of Scylla. Today we face a turning point. More emphasis on Scylla, at the expense of Charybdis, gains companies very little.

Seeing this, a few companies have moved into the center channel, their sails catching the winds. These companies lead, pulling ahead of the ships that hug the shore. Others too are leaning on their tillers, coming about, heading for open seas, regaining their long forgotten balance.

❖ **Developing an engaged, humane, and open work culture means seeking a balance.**

THE TWO HALVES OF YOUR ORGANIZATION'S CULTURE

Think of culture as a circle. The bottom is Scylla, the operations half, *what* we do, the hardware, systems, controls, production, and profits. On the top is Charybdis, the human half, *how* we do operations—with meanings, communications, trust, relationships, and involvement. A well-developed work culture balances both halves.

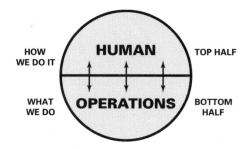

THE BALANCED WORK CULTURE

Open, balanced company cultures are highly productive because they allow people to bring more of themselves to work.

Most company cultures have a well-developed bottom half, but their top is underdeveloped.

THE UNBALANCED WORK CULTURE

For most organizations, the *what* is often given to them by technology, customers, markets, laws, etc. The greatest flexibility lies in *how* they will get it done. Meaning, values, attitudes, trust, and motivation come more from *how* things are done than from *what* is done. The opportunity lies in *how* we do things.

❖ **It is the company's culture that delivers, or does not deliver.**

❖ **Because they can manage how things are done, leaders can manage the work culture.**

SPLITTING—ANALYSIS AND SYNTHESIS

Analysis breaks down complex issues into parts and examines each part. Synthesis holds things together in their relationship or puts back together things that were taken apart; it includes holding equally the two sides of a true dilemma, something you cannot do with analysis.

Corporate leaders do not need more analysis. In fact, excessive analysis is part of the work culture problem. What leaders search for is synthesis, holding together and growing large, complex systems. Understanding your company culture is not an analytic activity; it is mostly a synthetic activity, something you *do* more than something you *think about*.

Using analysis to look at whole complex human issues in simplistic, or "scientific" ways, is called splitting. Splits separate things—events from experience, the human from the operational. In less mature work cultures you often hear issues posed as splits, as either-or questions or statements. "Do you want this or that?" "Well it either is or is not OK with you."

Splitting, a powerful defense against intimacy, is a destructive aspect of Western society and of organizational culture. Splitting is a daily experience for each of us. If we treat someone like an object, or if people treat us like objects, we are part of a split. Here are some common splits:

Thinking . . . . . . Feeling
Mind . . . . . . Body
Personality . . . . . . Experience
Work . . . . . . Pleasure
Culture . . . . . . People
Analysis . . . . . . Synthesis
Action . . . . . . Experience
Management . . . . . . Labor
Boss . . . . . . Subordinate
World . . . . . . Myself

☞ A cultural leader encourages discussions of whole events and context, not divided parts. On anything but simple subjects, stay away from abstract, academic, or theoretic talk. As you think and talk, stay with what is real, stay with the whole situation and your experience of it. Encourage others to discuss their experiences, not abstracted parts, conclusions, or events without context. Keep things whole and together.

Companies often encourage splits by inappropriately applying analysis, an essential part of the bottom half of their culture, to the human or top half of their culture.

Here is one common split: As you begin opening the work culture, some managers will say, "I don't have time for that touchy feely stuff" (as if feelings are not part of the workplace) or "Just tell me what you want. Do you want results, or do you want everyone involved?" (as if involvement and results are not complementary). By presenting an either-or question, they are pulling you into a split, echoing the call of Scylla, the hard, tough, analytic.

☞ Do not respond directly to this call. Do not argue or debate. Do not feed, escalate, or enlarge the split.

Try to respond in an integrative way: "It is not an either-or issue. We are responsible for creating a human *and* productive workplace. We must hold together people and operations. (To reinforce the point, you might clasp your hands together.) I will help you do that. Now, let's talk about the situation. Tell me what happened."

Splits are bad for you, your family, your people, your organization, and your profitability. Splits lurk in every nook and cranny of your organization. Be watchful.

WHO ARE CULTURAL LEADERS?

It is not possible to develop an organization's culture without courageous leadership—courageous because the powerful pull of the existing work culture makes it dangerous to step outside of the norms. How leaders act to support cultural development makes all the difference. Changing your company culture cannot be delegated.

Leaders guide by showing the way for others to follow. A cultural leader is the person who, by example, balances human values alongside work tasks. These leaders can be at any level—they can be the president or highest manager in the unit, a supervisor, or a non-manager. Cultural leaders make it clear how people and operating issues can be held together. When a person or group begins to talk from only the bottom half of the culture, as if people do not exist, the cultural leader gently adds the missing top half, the human side.

Leaders look like you and me because they *are* you and me. We are all leaders. If you are not an executive manager, it may seem dangerous to take the cultural lead. When you are below deck, winds gusting, and someone else's hand is on the tiller, it may not seem possible to wrest control of the vessel. But you can ask questions in any meeting and you can influence your own work group. "Have we talked this over with the people affected?" or "I know we need to move quickly, but are we sure the department is ready yet?"

Most people want to have a good day, feel competent, be productive, enjoy their work, and have good relationships. If you give people half a chance by setting an example with how you do your everyday work, how you lead, they will rise to join you.

That is cultural leadership.

LEADING TODAY'S EMPLOYEES

Today's employees want more of a say in what goes on around them. They want to be communicated with and listened to, have their opinions considered, and participate in decisions that affect them. Employees at all levels have become less responsive to traditional narrow-range, directive, uncommunicative, and sometimes punitive leadership, which they see as weak.

Great leaders have always responded with vision and flexibility to the needs of the people who follow them. People want to be engaged. Today's strong leaders develop an engaging work culture by doing two essential things.

▶ **Creating the Right Environment:** being role models themselves, encouraging and rewarding those who show new leadership behavior. Leaders do this by being open and receptive in discussions, discussing human values in conversations and meetings, and celebrating and rewarding people who demonstrate desired cultural values, leaving no doubt as to appropriate behavior.

▶ **Installing the Right Processes:** providing formal processes and guidance for participation in decisions, so that people at all levels can contribute to decisions that affect them.

This new leadership is receptive, open, cooperative, participative, communicative, win-win. These leaders provide clear vision, goals, directions, limits, boundaries, and stability. They reward success, seeing failures as opportunities for learning. Above all, these leaders see that participation and good communications depend on a network of personal relationships based on understanding and respect.

❖ **This kind of leadership creates organizations that engage people at work. These company cultures are highly productive.**

HIGH PRODUCTIVITY IS EASY

In a year your consultation cost us one day of can lids, and plant productivity has gone up 40%. —Plant manager

Late one night a police officer came across a drunk down on his hands and knees under a street light, searching carefully. "What are you doing?" "Looking for my keys." "Did you lose them here?" "No I lost them down the street, but this is where the light is."

This joke illustrates a commonplace situation in organizations. Conventional logic says if you want to increase productivity, focus on it, but this rarely works because the focus may not be where the problem is. Ironically, more pressure on operations may increase stress and decrease productivity.

People know what to do to increase production. Lack of training or information is rarely the problem. The problem is getting rid of what is blocking them from doing it.

If people feel they are objects, expenses, accessories to production, you can hardly expect them to give all that they can. On the other hand, if they feel they are the subject, the focus of what happens, if they feel you care, then they will care about you and the system. Employees know very well what to do. In a caring context, productivity comes easily.

This does not mean that efforts at the human level can compensate for something wrong at the hardware level (such as seriously obsolete equipment) or at the market level (such as a declining industry). But if the operations are in reasonable shape, the highest leverage is at the human level.

American companies that create engaging, humane and open work cultures are experiencing productivity gains beyond anything achievable by other means. I have seen productivity jumps from 10-40% over three years, the result of a new approach to everyday work by existing leaders. You do not need to add anyone or anything new. Just do what you have to do in a balanced way.

TO UNDERSTAND CULTURE, TRY TO CHANGE IT

You get to know an organization's culture as you get to know a person, by doing things together and gradually learning about each other—what it likes and does not like, what it will and will not do. You might say a company's culture is best known by the ways it responds to efforts to change it. In fact, changing a work culture is the only way to understand it.

You cannot understand an organization's culture through analysis. Like people, organizational cultures cannot be modeled, categorized, stereotyped, or described except in superficial ways. Language, as a creation of people, cannot fully describe people or an organization's culture.

Earlier we said that if you want to understand an event, look at the situation, the setting. Company cultures are what they are because of their setting. A work culture's setting is its history, marketplace, larger society, the personalities of the founder, board, senior management, and more. These elements set the cultural stage for what everyone does.

We each have a wide variety of behaviors available. In a single day we can be adults or like children, we can mentor an employee and be mentored. Organizational cultures also move about, sometimes quite mature, sometimes like adolescents. All work cultures have room to develop—and should. With your help, they will. A humane, open, mature work culture is essential for the creativity and engagement of employees, for the viability of the organization, and for stockholder profitability.

❖ **Start with something small, and watch the effect. Learn about your culture by doing things with it—step by step.**

Cultural evolution is the ascent of man.
    —Jacob Bronowski, *The Ascent of Man*

The Development of Culture

A culture's development and a person's development follow similar paths. You can say that culture is personality written large. Culture affects—even creates—an individual's personality. How and where we were raised greatly influences who we are and what we do. Cultures pull from us certain behaviors while inhibiting others. An open, humane, work culture nurtures involvement and mature behavior from all employees.

Frank, a production line operator in a Western plant, had a corporatewide reputation as a real troublemaker. For more than fifteen years, he directed his considerable intelligence and energy against the company at two locations.

Frank volunteered to join a "Quality Circle." Perhaps he saw a new vehicle for attack. Managers were apprehensive. Six months later, Frank was the circle's strongest advocate. He spoke proudly of increased line efficiency and reduced product loss, saying "I never had a good place to put my frustrations. Now I do."

With several other employees, he traveled to corporate headquarters, making an impassioned appeal for more employee involvement. Vice presidents who knew the old Frank could hardly believe it was the same person. He was. It was the work culture that changed.

Organizational culture, personality, and experience

As we saw in Chapter 1, a company's culture is the stage for human behavior and experience. What people do tells us about the cultural field. Just as scientific facts are revealed by external observation and physical measurement, cultural facts are revealed by human behavior and experience. Our own experience is the true data on our company's culture.

Our actions do not always reveal and often indeed hide our experience. The "real me" is private, unique, and largely secret (certainly to others and often to me). We may do something because it is "the right thing," what is expected in a situation. We may be in a meeting and feel like saying something but do not. We may like what someone says but not compliment them.

Our experience, the mix of meanings (thoughts, hopes, fears, and joys) and actions (what we say and do), makes up who we are. In many organizations, people often talk as if external objects and events are reality, as if people's experiences were abstractions and not real. Our experience is the most immediate and vivid thing we know. You might even say experience is reality (even if the company culture might not let you say this out loud).

Our experience, who we are, is made from whole cloth. We cannot change or replace pieces of our experience or our personality as if we were machines. Our experience is also inseparable from the situation. Responding to a situation is not necessarily a rational act, it is far more complex. Sometimes we embarrass ourselves or behave in "justifiable" ways: "I shouted at her because she made me mad. She talks the way my mother always talked." Whatever our reasons, we sense the situation and respond accordingly. From our point of view, our actions are always appropriate. If you see a person's behavior only as a problem, you miss what they are telling you about the situation, the work culture, and the leadership.

❖ **What people do contains information about the organization's culture and leaders.**

❖ **If people are engaged and responsible, it is because the work culture permits it.**

MATURITY

Work cultures develop and mature by moving up the same ladder that people do, each step adding new experience and dimensions. Cultural development, maturing, and evolution are three descriptions of the same path.

To use a human analogy: At birth our physical body pre-occupies us—warmth, food, being held, sleep. As we become aware of ourselves as individuals, we must learn to relate first to parents, then to outsiders. By junior high school, we are absorbed with trying to conform to our peer group.

By college, we are looking at others as models to see who we want to be as adults. By our mid-twenties, if we are lucky, we have experienced competence in some field, and are able to move on, exploring independence, building our life, walking our own path.

Maturity is not easily defined. It is complex, its meaning varying from country to country. Below are some American measures of maturity, expressed as extreme ends of the continuous journey, for an organization's culture and for people. Other countries might add and delete items. For example, in Eastern cultures, "face," reticence, obedience, and cooperation might appear on the list.

IMMATURE CULTURE	MATURE CULTURE
Dependent	Interdependent
Control by others	Self control
Motivated by others	Self motivated
Passive	Active
Short time perspective	Long time perspective
Subordinate position	Superordinate position
Unaware of "self"	Aware of "self"
Fearful, defensive	Accepting, outgoing
Exploits others	Supportive, interactive
Conceptual confusion	Conceptual clarity
Conceptual simplicity	Conceptual complexity
Wishes	Creates
Impulsive	Integrated

CULTURAL DEVELOPMENT—MATURING

The development scale below (Loevinger and Wessler) is a good way to describe our Western process of cultural maturing. "Development" means moving from "Impulsive" through "Integrated." Organizational cultures contain the potential for each stage. Most stand arrested at the "Self-Protective" and "Conformist" patterns.

Impulsive. Fear of retaliation, dependent, exploitive, aggressive, stereotyped behavior, conceptual confusion.

Self-Protective. Fear of being caught, externalizing blame, opportunistic, wary, manipulative, exploitive, self-protecting. Wishes advantage and control.

Conformist. Following external rules, shame, guilt for breaking rules, belonging, helping, superficial niceness, concern for appearance and acceptability, banal feelings and behavior, conceptual simplicity. Uses stereotypes and clichés.

Conscientious. Self-evaluated standards, self-criticism, guilt for consequences, long-term goals and ideals, intensive, responsible, concern for communication, understands feelings and motives for behavior, self-respect for achievements, traits, and expression, conceptual complexity, patterning.

Autonomous. Add to "Conscientious," coping with conflicting inner needs, tolerance, respect for the autonomy of others, vividly conveyed feelings, integration of thought and action, clear role, self-fulfillment, sees self in a social context, increased conceptual complexity, complex patterns, tolerates ambiguity and paradoxes, broad scope, and objectivity.

Integrated. Add to "Autonomous," reconciling inner conflicts, lets go of unattainable, values individuality, clear identity.

❖ **Cultural leadership means helping the organization incorporate more of the higher stages.**

CULTURAL MATURITY AND PRODUCTIVITY

Although individuals within a group may be very mature, most groups behave immaturely, low on the developmental scale.

Cultures are groups. While cultures contain all potential ranges of behavior, one pattern usually dominates. This is often the "Self-Protective," or "Conformist" patterns described on the previous page. Members of the work culture, responding appropriately to the field, stay within that pattern even if outside the organization's culture they behave differently.

By developing a more mature and engaging work culture, you tap into what people can bring. This is the opportunity.

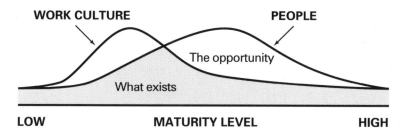

An organization culture, dominated by an early stage of maturity, usually frustrates leaders. Fortunately change lies in leadership's hands. People do not want to behave immaturely. If they see cultural leaders asking through their actions for more maturity, they will quickly comply, sometimes behaving more maturely than their leader.

FINDING PEACE WITH AUTHORITY

Coming to terms with authority is part of maturing. Authority has several meanings. One is the legitimate authority we give social institutions such as a traffic signal, our president, or an organization. Another is an emotional meaning we learn as children with our controlling parents.

We experience the controlling nature of authority from our earliest days, first with mother, then father, older siblings, neighbors, teachers, the military, and employers. Many of us remember how an angry parent caused our heart to pump, our adrenaline to flow. These childhood experiences stay with us. A similar situation activates the old feelings.

If we are lucky, as we age we may let go of seeing our parents as authority figures and see them experiencing their lives much as we do—loving, laughing, crying. We may also begin seeing outside authority figures such as employers in a similar way, not as dominating, not as fear-inspiring, but as ordinary people in a special role.

Becoming an adult means becoming your own parents, finding peace with authority. This is true of organizations: A company culture at peace with authority is very mature.

Structured authority is an essential part of every organization and society. It clarifies tasks, explains the big picture, and allows people to work together without treading on each other's toes or duplicating effort. The structure of authority can allow people to tap into their full talents. It can also stifle these talents.

Most of us are ambivalent towards authority. We like the structure because it gives us freedom. We hate the structure because it controls us. As an adult we want to be free of restrictions. So we are ambivalent.

We cannot escape authority. To come to terms with it, gently embracing our ambivalence, is a sign of maturity.

❖ **How leaders manage authority affects how far, how well, and how fast their organization's culture will develop.**

FIVE WAYS WE RELATE TO AUTHORITY

1. **Fight it**. We can struggle against authority. We may do this mentally, or by how we discuss the authority, or we may talk back to it. We may openly attack authority—put railroad spikes in ancient redwood trees, or march in demonstrations. Fighting is a typical pre-adult (teenage) response.

2. **Flee from it**. We can let our minds "drift out the window" or leave physically. Some people go so far as to live alone in the wilderness . . . or become consultants.

3. **Identify with it**. If the authority is humane, we will be humane. If it is aggressive, we will be aggressive. Aggression is very common in organizations, between departments, between management levels, or between supervisors and union employees.

4. **Obey it**. All work cultures depend on rules and obedience to authority to function. A society without laws is not a society. Simple obedience to authority—stopping at a stop sign—is the most common response.

5. **Let go of it**. This response is more mature than the first four. *Letting go* means growing beyond experiencing authority as controlling. For this person, authority does not exist as an issue.

On the outside this last response often looks like number four, but it is different in experience and meaning. A person who has let go does not fear higher authority because he or she does not experience authority as higher or lower, but simply as another institution or person in another role. Authority no longer has an emotional connotation. These people have found peace with authority; they have become their own parents.

❖ **The strong field of authority in hierarchical organizations draws out all these responses—particularly the first four.**

AUTHORITARIANISM

A vice president in a 20,000-person retail company was telling me how much he liked Jack, a department manager, and how valuable he was. I suggested he tell Jack. Just then Jack walked by and the VP said "I think I'll keep you." As authoritarians often do, he changed an opportunity to build a relationship* into a situation where he could reinforce his control.

Authoritarianism is a dominant and destructive pattern in many organizations. While true authoritarians are only 5% of our population, they hold a disproportionate number of key positions in corporations. If you have worked for an authoritarian boss, you know how it feels—and you probably hated it.

Do not confuse authoritarianism with decisiveness and authoritativeness. An authoritarian boss withholds information and controls outcomes. The authoritative boss gives relevant information to help his people decide what to do.

Last century and early this century, we saw how authoritarians achieve success. Great railroad barons and bankers left us an essential American infrastructure while assembling great personal and corporate wealth built on a trail of human wreckage.

As society has matured, we find these characters increasingly unacceptable, either as leaders of state or of organizations. We ask and expect more from leaders. Today the phrase "Winning is not the main thing, it is the only thing" has a hollow ring. Remember President Nixon and Watergate?

Authoritarian behavior is very common in organizations. Organizations are pyramidal, like families stacked on top of each other, parents over children. This structure sets the stage for an authoritarian work culture that encourages authoritarian behavior from each person in it.

Most authoritarian behavior is a response to the company culture. The only way you can tell if a person is a deep-seated authoritarian is to develop the culture. As the culture development train leaves the station, most people will get on board, but 5-10% will not.

---

* The opportunity to build a relationship is never lost. The VP can still talk with Jack at any time.

What distinguishes full-blown authoritarians is how strongly they resonate in a work culture that emphasizes control. Authoritarians have a deep-seated need to control. You might say they have to behave that way. They enjoy dominating people.

Most of us see a given work situation as a problem to be solved. The authoritarian sees situations as something to control. He does not understand win-win solutions, only win-lose, and he has to win. He believes might makes right. His view has to dominate. If it does not, he feels he has lost.

Because he has such a need to dominate, he will put much energy into "winning." In the face of such exaggerated behavior, most of us stand aside, allowing authoritarians to take charge. We are not weak. We simply do not enjoy fighting as much as they do.

You may never meet someone with all the characteristics of a full-blown authoritarian like Hitler or General Patton, although you have probably met people who display many such attributes. At times, we all show some authoritarian qualities as part of the normal palette of human behaviors.

Authoritarians are submissive and obedient to those above and dictatorial and aggressive to those below. For authoritarians, there is no middle ground, only above-below, superior-inferior. Those above see a good soldier, obeying instructions. Those below see a brutal, rigid boss. There seem to be two people in one body.

Such managers crave simple answers to complex questions: "Well, it either is or it isn't. Just say 'yes' or 'no'."

Underlying what looks like a tough manager is a terrified child, fearful of showing caring and openness, which he thinks is weakness. Suppressing this infantile fear, maintaining a wall of defenses, takes much energy. Drained by this, authoritarians are often tired, tense, and humorless. Their rigidity leaves little room for creativity.

Authoritarians like predictable settings where they can exercise control over "deviants." They feel threatened by democratic, participatory organizations. They are intolerant of flexible, risk-taking, open work cultures.

Because authoritarians see open behavior (vulnerability) as weakness, they respond by stamping it out. Fearful of loss of control, they stifle open discussions, pushing for simple, hasty decisions.

☞ Confront deep-seated authoritarians at their own level with a display of power (your own forceful control). Be firm and direct about your intentions to develop a humane, open work culture. Authoritarians are experts at fighting. Do not fight. If your boss is authoritarian, interview him or her. Build a relationship that moves away from stereotyping and battles.

As a consultant, some of my most difficult situations have been in a division with an open, creative leader but an authoritarian culture at corporate headquarters. Lower managers look up and see a confusing picture. They do not know which style to follow. Should they involve people or should they kick ass?

Ninety-five percent of authoritarian behavior reflects the organization's culture. A carefully managed work culture will not encourage these destructive patterns.

❖ **Authoritarian work cultures produce authoritarian behavior.**

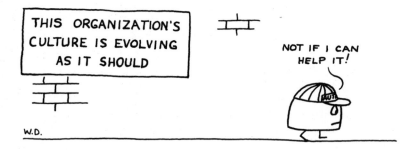

PERSONALITIES LIMIT CULTURAL DEVELOPMENT

As people learn to balance the human and operational halves, performance rises. As people become more open to caring for others and to others' involvement, trust increases. As trust and relationships improve, so does understanding. Better communications, information, and teamwork follow. Cooperative behavior replaces fighting. People listen more. Decisions improve. On such an engaging stage, it is no wonder productivity jumps.

Sadly all is not well in this promised land. The trolls of authoritarianism are lurking in the shadows. They have watched the increasing openness with concern. As it encroaches on their sacred territory, control, they begin to growl loudly. If they are important trolls, they will not be ignored. Employees understand these limits well. They push, but not too hard. Bravery is foolishness. Most of us have experienced how authoritarians set limits on productivity.

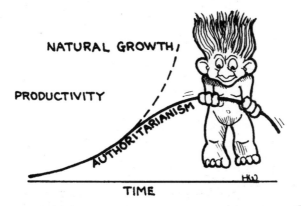

NATURAL GROWTH

PRODUCTIVITY

AUTHORITARIANISM

TIME

AUTHORITARIANISM LIMITS PRODUCTIVITY

As a society, we do not have enough experience developing organizational cultures to know where the upper limits of productivity are. There may be none. We do know that when other parts of the system are in good shape, the limits are not set by ordinary people but by those who cannot tolerate a developed open work culture.

Synergy means behavior of whole systems
unpredicted by behavior of their parts.
 —R. Buckminster Fuller, *What I Have Learned*

Groups and Systems

Cultural leaders guide groups and systems, not individuals. Groups act as wholes, as more than the sum of the people in them. Groups have a way of their own. Groups (but not necessarily the individuals in them) act in rather primitive, often child-like, but understandable ways.

We have all experienced groups—family, school, college. At work, we belong to many groups; a department, peers, lunch friends, a special project, outside vendors, professional associations, or a union. We are skilled at moving between groups, behaving appropriately and differently in each.

Groups can be fun, frustrating, productive, wasteful, time consuming, and time saving, all in the space of a few minutes.

To understand a group or culture you are in, pay attention to your experiences and feelings. If you are feeling satisfied, energetic, tense, fearful, confused, frightened, angry, elated, or alienated, that is good data about the state of the group. Sharing your experience with the group helps it be more self-aware and mature.

What follows is some group theory. Like the language of culture, the language of groups is like the language of personality.

EARLY STAGES OF WORK GROUPS

A new group, like an infant, sees wisdom and knowledge in its leader. Members expect the leader to be an authority, to give the group wisdom. New groups are like empty vessels, expecting leaders to fill them. This expectation is very apparent during the early minutes of a first meeting, particularly if there is little pre-meeting information. Members may seem almost mindless.

There is no way leaders can measure up to these unrealistic subconscious expectations. No matter what the leader does, some members will gradually become hostile. They will criticize and confront the leader, directly or indirectly. At the same time, others will become subconsciously anxious, afraid that the leader will punish the group. They try to rescue the leader by offering support.

If the group's anger at the leader's imagined withholding of information becomes too strong, the group may avoid its true target (the leader) and argue internally. Members may also choose to ask disarming or irrelevant questions, usually about technical content or subjects that deflect attention from the true feelings of the group: "Did you use the old program or the current version?" or "What are our lunch plans?"

By asking such nonthreatening questions, the group avoids its hostility to the leader. Some members will go further by trying to set up the leader as a wise person, getting her to lecture to the group. At this point, it is common for unwary leaders to trap themselves by directly answering people's questions or by talking too much. If the leader does either, the group will become increasingly disappointed and passive, or it might explode with hostility.

☞ Group leaders should turn back questions, getting members to assume responsibility. "How do you think we should approach this problem? Should we tackle our cost problems first or our declining productivity?" Be dependable without causing dependence. Use a clear decision process. Hold members responsible for content.

When a group recognizes its own wisdom, it will no longer expect to receive special knowledge from its leader and can discuss the real issues. Members will then become responsible participants instead of receptacles. As it matures, with its leader's help, the group will question agendas, look at issues, set priorities, and assign work.

Group behavior depends on personal relationships between participants. When personal relationships are weak or stereotyped, competitive behavior dominates. You often see this in labor-management or interdepartmental meetings. In these meetings, people do not see others as colleagues, but as opponents, as stereotypes. They will then act out these stereotyped roles.

When relationships are weak, people in power will behave to keep their rank. Subordinates will show their competence or outdo a competitor. Others will posture, showing they are not afraid of authority or demonstrating their independence.

Overcome this by developing personal relationships and team decision making. When people see each other as allies, as human beings instead of as titles, when they experience the power of collaborative decisions, they will relate to each other more openly and maturely.

❖ **Most people are more mature than the groups they join. The culture makes groups behave immaturely. Leaders can change this.**

THE ICEBERG OF CONSCIOUSNESS—
GROUPS AND PEOPLE

Consciousness is like an iceberg, mostly hidden beneath the surface. Rational organizational tasks are visible. Next are politics, some discussed, some not, then our private thoughts and feelings. Lower still are the preconscious and subconscious. Most of what goes on in us, and in groups, is unconscious.

About 20% of communication is verbal. Logic is perhaps 20% of that. Sometimes we talk as if rationality is a large part of work life, even though our experience tells us differently.

A mature group is open and trusting, talking about deeper, meaningful things, such as organizational politics and personal (and always dominant) agendas, reasons, fears, and hopes. You can encourage this by discussing your personal experiences with the group.

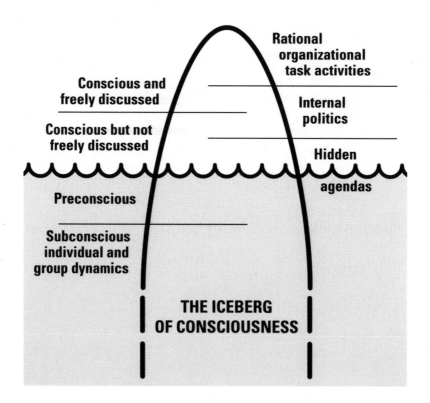

WAYS GROUPS AVOID WORK

Since World War II, the Tavistock Institute in London has studied groups. Researchers found that few groups stay at their task for long, but are often unaware that they have gone off track. These work-avoiding patterns fall into four general categories:

1. **Dependency.** Members act as though they know nothing. They will not give their leader information because "She knows everything." The group is silent, its leader frustrated, talking too much, drained, trapped, and angry.

2. **Fight or Flight.** This group either attacks a person or group, who may or may not be present, or runs away. Often it blames others for its problems or is passive, as if there is nothing the group can do about its situation.

3. **Pairing**. Two people in the group (usually the senior person and a bright young star) do all the talking. Others look on expectantly. However if the pair come up with a good idea, the others usually kill it, either in the meeting or later.

4. **Fusion.** Members feel they are part of a great group that can do anything. They deny internal differences, acting as though everyone likes everyone else. Members try to merge with the group, joining in the euphoria of shared action.

☞ If your group seems to be dependent on you or blaming others, if you and one other person are dominating, or if members are denying their real differences, the group may have fallen into one of these patterns.

These patterns are unconscious. When a member realizes what the group is doing and says so, after some discussion the group usually gets back on track.

A "STRONG" GROUP IS A WEAK GROUP

The lady doth protest too much, methinks. —W. Shakespeare, *Hamlet*

A hospital director was discussing difficulties in bringing together the hospital's administration, nurses, and doctors. "They each have such strong traditions and positions. They won't cooperate."

Exaggeration reveals a shadow side. For example, exaggerated strength reveals the weakness behind it, hence the need to put so much energy into maintaining defensive walls. True strength, true maturity, includes the ability to be open to individuality and diversity in other groups and people and to hold life's dilemmas open and unresolved.

The behavior this director described is the "Self-Protective" stage of cultural development (page 22). This stage is opportunistic, exploitive, and wary.

Behind the bravado of any tough, strong, position lurks fear. Faced with such behavior, leaders should be compassionate, helping individuals or groups rise above their arrested situation.

☞ Your role as leader of a strong (= weak) group, or person, is to be dependable without increasing dependence. Provide security, be clear about direction, reassure that the journey is a safe one, and ask questions that coach groups or individuals through their decision process. Provide structure but not answers. Mentor the "strong" child out of fearful defensiveness into an open, interactive, mature position. Take your time, perhaps several months of caring guidance.

TWO MEANINGS OF POWER

When we say someone has power we can mean:

▶ Power over people (control).

▶ Power to get things done—as in scientific usage where power is the ability to do work.

These two meanings often coincide in traditional organizations. But in today's emerging corporate cultures power is more often used to mean the ability to do work. A powerful person is someone who knows how to create an engaging culture that allows people to get more done.

☞ As a cultural leader, your words and actions direct those below to use power as either control or involvement. Choose your words and actions as carefully as you plan your schedule. Use words that set the stage for real power—for work, not for excessive control. For example do not say "impact" (hard, analytic) when you could say "relate to" (more integrative) or "problem" (narrow) when you could say "situation" (broad). Ask questions such as, "What do the people in your department think about this?" "Have you checked this out with the other departments affected?" See also "Leading by asking questions," page 86.

The most effective control is self-control at the lowest possible level. That comes when you push authority and traditional control down, not from retaining it on high.

As one department manager said after he had worked for several years learning to pass control down to his people, "I have more control now when I am away from the plant than I had before when I was on-site."

CONTROL

There are two general meanings of control.

Control by others

If we feel controlled, the field is probably dominated by competition, we are losers, someone else calls our shots. This field includes dominance, win-lose, politics, and using or abusing the power of position. It is a cultural field where people experience danger if they are too open, fear for their job or job growth, and suffer from lack of trust and support for who they are and what they are doing.

Self-Control

This means mastery of ourselves and the situation. It feels good to have our situation under control. This is the feeling we would like everyone to have in life and at work. This experience brings out the best in people, focusing their energy on work, on being productive, satisfying everyone.

Leaders who feel isolated from production may compensate by exerting the first type of control, control of others. They may clamp down on operations, impose excessive monitoring or indexing, or make threats: "Managers will be held accountable for a 10% decrease in costs by 1995," meaning "You will be fired if you don't get the numbers."

In contrast, if leaders experience a close relationship with employees, if they trust people, they will know that people want to experience the second type of control—self-control.

As people sense that leaders are asking for self-control, they will respond. Self-control quickly brings operations and production process under control. Costs drop and productivity rises.

The cultural "Interview" described on page 58, directly builds relationships and trust, which encourages self-control.

LEADERS LEAD SYSTEMS

It all hangs together.

Gerry managed an 800-person continuous production line plant. Over three years, he had put in place a structure that deeply involved the employees. Sensing the stage was now set, he appealed to his people to increase production. Within three months, they responded by raising productivity 40%. It stayed up.

Gerry is a very thoughtful manager, watching the effects of his actions on the whole system. He balances analysis (taking apart) on the lower, operations half with synthesis (holding together) on the top, human half. He carefully influences the whole plant by how he does everyday activities.

An excellent analyst, Gerry also sees his plant in a holistic, non-analytic way. He understands it as a "general system."

Characteristics of a general system:

▶ **A general system has subsystems that share the characteristics of the larger system.** A department is a general system because, like the whole organization, it has people, financial systems, and customers. This is also true of the next level up, the division. (In contrast, a person is a system, but not a general system—your parts do not have characteristics of your whole body: your arm does not think.)

▶ **A change in one part of the system affects the whole system.** All parts are related, none is isolated. Changing the interest rate affects every company in the nation and our relationship to international markets.

▶ **A balance between parts takes precedence over the individual excellence of any part.** This balance will always catch individual parts unprepared, incomplete, or in a state of some inefficiency. Even if each part of the system works as well as it can, the whole system will not work as well as it could. A car's parts must work in harmony and be appropriate to the car's purpose. If you maximize each part, the whole will be out of balance. It is the same with a production line. Maximizing each machine on the line guarantees the whole line will be unbalanced. The corollary: If you optimize a system you must run some parts below their optimum.

► **Evolution tells us that the characteristics of any system come mostly from the larger system of which it is a part.** General systems evolve through a relationship with the whole, with their environment. You cannot define or understand parts by only looking downwards at lower levels, subsystems, or events. To understand a system, you must look at the overall situation. To understand why a company makes what it makes, look at the marketplace. To understand an event, look at its context.

There is a big gap between the abstract analytic ideas we learned at school and the complexity of situations we face at work. Real life organizational problems are interconnected. Solutions require attention to facts and principles from many disciplines and many levels. Actions can never wait until all the facts are in.

Few managers make day to day decisions based on good systems thinking because the theories and models they learned leave out too much. Most managers look at parts, not at the whole or the context. Managers usually focus on events instead of interactions, relationships, and the situation.

For example, behavior (what you see, what someone does) is substituted for experience (the meaning and reason for the action), or the response to an integrative question like "What do you feel?" is often the analytic conclusion "I think...".

Understanding synthetic or integrative system thinking is hard work. Synthetic thinking is above analysis: it is impossible to capture in writing. It is as much something you do—paying attention to your experience—as it is something you think about. It involves adding new levels to traditional analytic thinking. It is the only way leaders can feel they have their arms comfortably around the whole operation.

MOST PROBLEMS ARE SYSTEMS PROBLEMS

When things go wrong in organizations it is usually because there are problems with the work process, or the procedures. Most cultures cause people to focus on events, not on the process that led up to the event. Looking at processes means looking at the event's context, at relationships between people, departments, functions, levels, and the outside world. This is painful. In most work cultures, it is simpler to blame a person than to examine the system.

In a developed work culture, managers see events as information about the system. In developed work cultures, managers solve problems by changing the system rather than seeing the problem as a unique event or connected to a "problem" person.

As trust develops and cooperation increases, people begin to feel that other people's problems are also theirs. They no longer feel that "The hole is in your end of the boat so I am O.K." Now everybody is in the same boat. They care. Cooperation becomes a valued part of the work culture.

☞ When people come to you with a problem, ask questions that make them think about the context of the event.
"Describe the situation. What led up to it?"
"Events don't exist in isolation. Do we understand the process?"
"Could you have some people look into our procedure. Perhaps it needs to be thought through?"

Looking at the context is essential in reducing recurring time-related problems like production line waste, processing orders, or managing the Thanksgiving or Christmas workload.

The best people to examine the process and streamline it are those most involved with it. They know where the problems are and how to get other related people and departments involved in analyzing and changing the process.

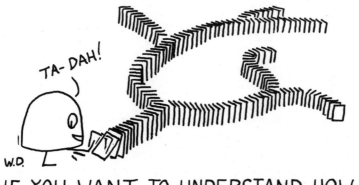

IF YOU WANT TO UNDERSTAND HOW A
SYSTEM WORKS, MAKE A CHANGE.

A DESK IS A DANGEROUS PLACE FROM WHICH TO VIEW THE WORLD

Action research—one small step at a time.

In 1947, Kurt Lewin introduced the idea of social action research. Simply put, the only way to understand a complex system is to make a small change and monitor its effects. To understand an organization's culture, make a change and watch how the system responds. This is the evolutionary approach.

This seems like common sense, yet we often act as though we can analytically predict results of planned actions at the human level just as we can predict how turning a dial will affect a machine. Companies lose billions of dollars annually because managers undertake large programs that fail. Bill Agee at Bendix Corporation attempted autocratic, quick, top-down culture change, insensitive to his people. He was fired. The press reports that Jack Welch at General Electric made billions by engaging people in a process of evolutionary change over many years.

Evolution is subtle, unpredictable, exciting, creative, open, and above all, responsive to its environment. Evolution does not take place behind a desk. You have to get out and mess about.

❖ **If you want to understand a work culture, make a change. The system will tell you about itself by how it responds.**

❖ **If you want to change a work culture, base the next step on the effects of the previous step.**

An isolated event is not an event.
        —Alfred N. Whitehead

Evolution and Culture

Cultures develop by evolving from lower to higher levels. Leadership means helping evolution. To most of us evolution means Darwin—survival of the fittest. But evolution also has a broader meaning, the developmental process from the beginning of matter to our present stage of human awareness.

Evolution is not a smooth process. Systems, like your organization, are stable for a long time, then take a big step. Evolution has taken five big steps since the beginning of time.

With all living things:

1. Physics, matter .... 12 billion years ago
2. Life .... 3.6 billion years ago
3. Competition .... 1 billion years ago

With the coming of humans two to three million years ago, we add:

4. Language .... 1 million–100,000 years ago
5. Experience, awareness ... 3,000 years ago

Your organization contains all these steps or levels, some more pronounced than others. Most organizational cultures have been blocked in reaching a naturally balanced state. Your role as leader is to remove the block so evolution will continue and all levels of the system will be in balance.

❖ **Developing your culture means removing the blocks, balancing each level**—easy to say, hard to do.

1. PHYSICS—FIRST STEP OF EVOLUTION

All rules and no forgiveness. –Joseph Campbell

Our universe began some 12 billion years ago. Matter gradually consolidated into galaxies and by 4 billion years ago, Earth was distinct.

Physical matter, its properties, and the rules that bind it are the first step of evolution. We know this level by gravity, acceleration, heat, sound, and electricity. If you run a car into a wall it is crushed—"for every action there is an equal and opposite reaction."

This first level of evolution is Newtonian, a world of certainty and pre-dictability, of hard science, concrete events, observation, facts, analysis, validation, and mathematics.

All organizations contain this level, sometimes in large ways (a chemical plant, warehouse, or shopping mall) sometimes in small ways (an office with phone, file cabinet, and computer). Large or small, the physical parts of the organization must run well or everything else suffers.

Equipment and the rules and principles of physics create the first level of evolution and of the organization, management, and leadership.

Words we associate with this level are:
Physics, chemistry, and engineering.
Hardware and equipment.
Analysis.
The facts of science.

2. LIFE—SECOND STEP OF EVOLUTION

And life is color, and warmth, and light.
                        —Julian Grenfell, *Into Battle*

About 3.6 billion years ago, when the earth had cooled sufficiently, an unexpected thing happened—life appeared, adding new system dimensions not conceivable from the first step of evolution.

The spark of life, the rules of systems and processes, the idea of interrelated and dependent system parts, feedback, and homeostasis: These do not exist in the world of physics.

As evolution walks its path, it does not leave levels behind, it just adds new ones. Life, systems, and processes do not abandon the rules of physics and chemistry. We cannot escape the field of gravity or leave our mass behind. There cannot be an event without physics.

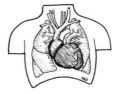

Words we associate with this level are:

Life, biology.
Functions and processes. Training.
Operating systems, which make "hardware" pieces work together as a system —for example, our body, a chemical plant, software, a transportation system.
Efficiency.

3. COMPETITION—THIRD STEP OF EVOLUTION

Don't get mad, get even. – bumper sticker

We do not know when competition first appeared on our planet, when survival of the fit became survival of the fittest. We do know that competition for resources was an established part of our landscape when the first simple animals appeared one billion years ago.

You may have some personal images for "competition"—amoebas eating bugs, *Tyrannosaurus rex* threatening an early mammal, the Prussian Empire dominating Europe, democracy, price wars, our stock market.

Just as life added a new dimension to physics, so competition added a new dimension that was not part of the two earlier levels. Competition is invisible from the levels of physics and systems.

Competition marches to a new, more complex, and sometimes strange drumbeat. This third level of evolution dominates the marketplace—and most organizations, leaving the work culture severely unbalanced.

Some words we associate with this level are:

Competition, markets, economics.
Authority, control, "power", dominance, behavior.
Rules, law, formal religions, politics, win-lose, democracy.
Information, decisions, logic.
Sociology, anthropology, philosophy, ethics.
Productivity, profits.

4. LANGUAGE—FOURTH STEP OF EVOLUTION

The pen is mightier than the sword. —E. L. Richelieu

While many animals communicate through movement, sounds, or smells, humans alone developed abstract systems, using physical and oral symbols to represent objects, events, and experiences.

One million years ago, we had words, perhaps 100,000 years ago a language. Art followed. About 10,000 years ago, we formed fixed agricultural communities and developed a written language. Many early writings are commercial records, bills of sale.

From the rules and principles of physics, biology, or competition, you cannot understand that a symbol, sound, or mark stands for an object or tells a story. Language is distinctively human. It separates us from the first three levels.

Language moves beyond the zero sum, win-lose game of competition. Dialogue, understanding, relationships, communications, and meanings behind actions are all at this level and all critical to an organization's success.

This is the most underdeveloped area of your company's culture. This is the level cultural leaders must focus on. This is the big opportunity.

Some words we associate with this level are:
Language, symbolic systems, communication.
Understanding, listening, meaning.
Relationships, consensus, teamwork.
Win-win.

5. EXPERIENCE—FIFTH STEP OF EVOLUTION

*To be conscious that we are perceiving or thinking is to be
conscious of our own existence.* —Aristotle

The fifth and last level of evolution has no real name because it lies beyond language.

Since about 1,000 B.C. humankind has become increasingly self-aware, conscious that we are separate, feeling, sensing beings, different from other animals. Some call this self-awareness or self-consciousness the sacred aspect of humans, though sacred does not imply formal religion.

Initially we sensed we were no longer merged with the spirits of rocks and plants or the animals we hunted. The biblical metaphor of this transition to self awareness is Adam, who ate the apple: "Your eyes shall be opened, and you shall be as gods, knowing good and evil." With ancient Greeks, this consciousness brought myths, democracy, literature with feelings, poetry, morality. Since the age of enlightenment (18th century), we have sought our place in the world as mature, responsible, fulfilled beings, creating our own futures. We are still just at the beginning of this last step of evolution.

There is nothing beyond aware experience. This level contains everything important to us. This is our life at home and at work—trust, caring, love, being valued and involved. The quality of experience is what makes life worthwhile.

Some words we associate with this level are:
Experience, self-awareness, self-consciousness.
Feelings, fear, love, caring, trust.
Involvement, satisfaction, values, spirit.
The facts or reality of our experience.

THE FIVE LEVELS OF LOGICAL TYPES

These five levels of evolution are known as the five levels of logical types because there is a type of logic associated with each level distinct from that of the previous level. Higher levels contain previous levels but add something not understood from below. Parts of biology can be explained using physics and chemistry, but the tendency of a living system to maintain a steady state cannot. Life cannot be seen from physics, language cannot be seen from nonhuman levels. Self-awareness is invisible from language.

Another way of saying this is that you can look down the levels of culture with understanding but you cannot look up with understanding. The practical application is that you cannot deal with issues of a higher level using only the tools of a lower level. ("You can't get there from here.") Analytic models of science are inadequate for dealing with the subtlety and complexity of human experience.

Managers often try to use the logic of lower levels to attempt changes at higher levels in their organization's culture—and fail. This is where most top-down, system-wide Quality Improvement Programs ran aground. They applied directive rational processes to what are essentially human issues.

If you use only logic, analysis, controls, and directives, you cannot create a workplace that engages people, where there is trust and caring, and where people bring all of themselves to work. Lower level approaches are fine for installing equipment or financial systems, but they are inadequate for leading cultural change.

❖ **The five levels of evolution contain everything in your organization. They are the structure for a map of your organization's culture. They are the parts that every manager has to manage and every leader has to lead. Leadership means managing each of these levels.**

THE TOP HALF OF CULTURE
(HOW AND WHY WE DO IT)

5. EXPERIENCE–
**feelings, trust, fear, caring,
values, involvement, satisfaction.**

4. LANGUAGE–communications,
**listening, meaning, understanding,
relationships, teamwork, consensus, win-win.**

↕ ↕ ↕

3. COMPETITION–economics, authority,
**control, "power", dominance, politics, win-lose,
democracy, rules, laws, ethics, information,
productivity, profits, markets, decisions, behavior.**

2. LIFE–systems and processes, biology,
**operational procedures and methods,
training, software, efficiency.**

1. PHYSICS–chemistry, equipment,
**hardware, engineering,
technology.**

THE BOTTOM HALF OF CULTURE
(WHAT WE DO)

© Meridian Group, © 1985, 1996

THE CIRCLE OF CULTURE
THE FIVE LEVELS OF EVOLUTION,
CULTURE, AND LEADERSHIP

ORGANIZATIONAL CULTURES ARE UNBALANCED

Organizational cultures are strong in some areas, weak in others. Leadership means getting each level in balance.

5. EXPERIENCE—*feelings, trust, fear, caring, values, involvement, satisfaction*	There is always experience, but in most organizations the quality of it is poor. You cannot get to this directly, only through actions at level 4.
4. LANGUAGE—*communications, listening, meaning, understanding, relationships, teamwork, consensus, win-win*	This is the thinnest area in most organizational cultures. Communications, understanding, relationships, and teamwork, are usually weak. +
3. COMPETITION—*economics, authority, control, politics, win-lose, rules, information, productivity, profits, decisions*	Although not always discussed, openly, this level is overemphasized in most organizational cultures.
2. LIFE—*systems and processes, biology, operational procedures and methods, training, software, efficiency*	Operating systems are often poorly developed. There is usually plenty of room for process improvements.*
1. PHYSICS—*chemistry, equipment, hardware, engineering, technology*	In most organizations, this level is fine. It is easier to talk about equipment than the more productive areas of processes (2), or communications (4).

+ This is your biggest opportunity to develop the work culture.

* This is usually your next biggest opportunity. As you develop the work culture, people will tackle problems at this level.

❖ **Leadership means getting the levels in balance, thereby improving the quality of everyone's experience and the performance of the system.**

SUMMARY OF SECTION ONE

▶ An organization's culture is like a person: complex, interactive, developing, evolving, responding.

▶ A culture is a field of influences, affecting everyone and every thing. It is the stage for who we are and what we do, for success or for something else. Developing the company culture has very high leverage.

▶ By how they do their everyday activities, leaders determine how far and how fast the company's culture will develop.

▶ Because people respond to their environment, what people do tells you about the work culture and about its leadership.

▶ Company cultures naturally evolve. Developing the culture means removing what is blocking this natural evolution.

▶ You understand a work culture by doing things with it. Base your next step on the effects of the previous step.

▶ Most organizations are structured hierarchically. This encourages authoritarianism. Authoritarian cultures induce authoritarian behavior from everyone. Authoritarianism limits productivity.

▶ Balance in the whole system takes precedence over maximizing parts of the system. In a balanced system, some parts will be running below their capacity.

▶ Groups, but not necessarily the individuals in them, behave in undeveloped ways. Groups are systems. Systems respond to their environment. If you want to understand an event in a system, look to the environment.

▶ The most effective control is self-control, not top-down control. Real power is the ability to do work, to create an engaging company culture that allows people to get more done.

▶ You cannot change human areas using tools from nonhuman areas. Analysis, controls, and directives will not improve relationships, involvement, or attitudes,which make up the quality of experience and the basis for productivity.

Just Do It

Theory in Practice –Action-research

This section shows how theory leads to action.

Chapter 5—High leverage actions. Some of these actions that powerfully develop work cultures may be unfamiliar.

Chapter 6—The decision process. How you involve people in daily decisions makes all the difference.

Chapter 7—Regular activities. We will look at some familiar organizational actions from a cultural viewpoint.

A traditional operational manager focuses on the lower half of the culture, on operations: "We use people to solve problems." When you look at something from a cultural point of view you focus on the top half of culture, on people. "We use problems to involve people." Where you start says why you are doing it. It reveals your values, showing what you believe is most important, people or operations.

You can get to operations by starting with people, but you cannot get to people by starting with operations. It is one of those "You cannot get there from here" things.

With one approach you solve immediate problems while maintaining the existing work culture. With the other, you solve problems (usually better) and you advance the work culture; you change the cultural field. Then everything else in operations works better and other problems do not develop.

Do not expect grand plans or company wide programs. Develop your work culture with small successful actions.

❖ **Cultural leaders place people first. They know that operational excellence will then follow.**

*There is very little difference between one man and
another; but what little there is, is very important.*
— W. James, *The Principles of Psychology*

High Leverage Actions

The simplest and fastest way to develop the work culture is to
intervene directly at high levels of human experience. "The
Circle of Culture" on page 52 includes the following words
from the human levels, the top half: "trust, caring, listening, understanding, involvement, satisfaction, relationships, meaning."

Changing any of these powerfully affects organizations. If trust
improves, communications improve, department barriers drop, and
operational problems are quickly resolved. Changes at human levels
have very high leverage.

This chapter gives examples of some high leverage actions you
can take to quickly develop your organization's culture.

All the examples in this book grew from existing needs.
Solutions to problems reflected the organization's stage of development, what it was prepared to do. Setting the stage for each action
took months, working with managers, looking in the mirror, building relationships, discussing communications and meanings. If you
do not keep in mind that the context for each example was an evolutionary consciousness, then the examples might look like ordinary
organizational development events.

❖ **As a cultural leader, do not try to do too much too fast. Forcing
top-down change is the sure road to failure. Look for pockets
of readiness and encourage them. Develop the open and
humane work culture naturally from what people are doing
now. Water existing seeds. Support evolution.**

THE CULTURAL INTERVIEW

The most direct way to open the company culture is by getting to know your people personally, changing the quality of your relationships. A powerful and simple way to do this is by "interviewing" people. I have found that interviews by themselves are enough to transform a work culture. No other action is as effective as the  interview in helping leaders sense the cultural landscape. Make it the foundation for any effort to develop a humane and open work culture.

The interview originally grew from discussions among a group of supervisors who wanted to change a traditional employee evaluation process into a true two-way communication process. Since then, it has been developed and refined. It is a chance for people to talk about themselves, their background, experiences, and hopes.

Interviews change an organization's culture by building personal relationships, introducing new kinds of discussions and experiences into the workplace, and making cultural themes visible to management, which then responds appropriately.

The interview lasts about forty minutes to an hour and a half. It is held in a private place at work, at a restaurant over coffee or lunch, or just walking together around the facility. Schedule the interview in advance so that the person has time to think about it and plan their day's work. Do not hold the interview in your office. Neither person should sit behind a desk. The ideal arrangement is two people sitting in comfortable chairs, informally.

Getting to know someone more closely is very rewarding. Some managers become so enthusiastic that they do several interviews a week, urging their associates to do the same.

The following outline of the interview came from a group of supervisors in a unionized facility who had experienced its power.

What is the purpose of the discussion or interview?

It is one whole human being talking with another whole human being. It should be the kind of experience we would like to see more of in our company—open, inviting, friendly, confidential, and enjoyable. It is a time to step out of your usual role as information-giver or question-answerer. In the interview, you listen, understand, and build a relationship.

In the interview you:

Learn more about each other.
Open lines of communication.
Break down barriers.
Become more comfortable around each other.
Find a different side to each other.
Find common interests.
Listen to what is being said instead of talking.
Create better relationships.
Understand each other.
Hear ideas or suggestions.
Understand how others experience work.
  (It is not a problem solving discussion.
  It is not to discuss only work.)

The interview setting?

Let the person know well ahead of time the purpose of the interview: "To get to know each other better."
Find a convenient time for both of you.
Explain that it is confidential and say how long it will be.
Choose a neutral site (not your office), with no barriers such as a desk. No phone, no interruptions. Keep it private and confidential. Note pad if needed. Casual warm handshake, offer coffee.
Believe in it, be honest.
Be ready with your opening subject.
Finish with, "Thank you, I have enjoyed this."

☞ Sometimes the person will immediately start talking about work or a personal topic. If they do, just stay on that topic for a while. There is no one way to do an interview. Every interview, like every person, is different. Relax and go with the flow. Try to touch on something from each of the four general areas suggested below, but if you do not, that is O.K.

What are the conversation topics?

1. **Before** joining the company:
    How did you come to be with the company?
    What did you do before that? And before that?
    Childhood, school, where grew up?
    Parents, where from, occupations?
    Children, spouse, home, hobbies, weekends, vacations?
    What do you like people to know about you?
    What would you like to know about me?

2. **Future.** What I look forward to:
    How do you see things down the road?
    Future hopes, plans, work and nonwork?

3. **Work history with the company.** What I have done here:
    What was it like when you first came here?
    Work highlights over the years?

4. **Now.** Present work experiences, and what these mean:
    Tell me about your work now.
    Recent things that involved you? Recent experiences?
    What did these experiences mean to you?
    Tell me about communications? And relationships?
    What parts of your work do you enjoy the most?
    And what parts do you enjoy the least?
    What things here would you like to change?

The manager gently guides the topics and does not dominate the conversation. It is an opportunity for the employee to talk. Both should leave feeling satisfied.

Frequently a management team will do one interview each a week. This opens the company culture rapidly because the interview connects at the highest human level—experience and relationships.

The most difficult part of the interview is the role change. Most managers and supervisors see themselves as problem solvers, as advice and information givers. In the interview, imagine that you are talking with a stranger at a neighborhood barbecue, not an employee or subordinate. For example, if you are a manager and an employee asks you about a problem, you usually answer it. You would not do that at a barbecue. You would just chat.

This role change is most difficult when you are interviewing people who work for you in traditional relationships.

Most interviewing is downwards, with people in your own department. Sometimes managers and supervisors use it to open departmental lines, either horizontally or vertically. In each of the following cases, the interviewers started with a brief orientation and practice session on the interview.

▶ The clerks in a shipping and transportation department had problems with the purchasing department. Buyers would often change orders without notifying shipping. One of the clerks asked to meet with a buyer. She interviewed him, getting to know him better but not discussing work very much. Other clerks interviewed other buyers. The purchasing manager heard what was happening and stopped it. He called it a waste of time, but the interviews had already had an effect. Relationships had changed and work issues were now resolved more easily. Six months later, the clerks tried again. This time, the purchasing manager did not resist. He realized that things were working better between the departments, though he was not sure why.

▶ In an engineering consulting company, a young engineer interviewed the company owner. They discussed their backgrounds, experiences, and management philosophies. The owner had never talked about work in this open, undirected way. The interview led to many other meetings and discussions; the engineer eventually became influential in the management of the firm.

▶ The manager of a technical services department spent too much time in his office. Not enough information came down to the people in the department. Two employees decided to interview the manager. They took him to lunch. They thought it might be difficult to talk about nonwork topics, but it turned out to be O.K. The next week, the manager began strolling about the department, chatting with people. He kept this up, and the lack of information became history.

▶ When moving from one company to another, a vice president decided to use the interview as part of his entry strategy. He carefully planned to spend most of his first month interviewing employees, supervisors, and managers in the new company. Even though he came in to "turn around" the division, he wanted everyone to understand that he valued their ideas and experience. Though the demands of work made it difficult, he stayed the course. The result was a profound change in the culture over the following 18 months. Managers, supervisors, and union employees saw the new vice president as approachable, open to their ideas and suggestions. Managers and supervisors at the various plants in the division took up the baton, starting interviews themselves. A step change occurred in relationships. The problems the vice president came to solve slowly eased. Grievances and "lost time accidents" disappeared. Efficiency and profitability increased.

When you begin interviewing, people will naturally be suspicious. They might even ask "What is this about? Why do you want to talk with me?"

After you have interviewed several people, and they see that what you talked about was held in complete confidence, their feeling will change from suspicion to appreciation. This might happen during the interview. The person you are interviewing might suddenly relax and open up about personal areas—occasionally so personal that you might feel embarrassed.

You do not have to do anything about what people say in an interview. You are just two people, not a boss and subordinate. You are not gathering information, you are building a relationship. If you feel that you must act on what they say, ask their permission and agree on what you will say. This might happen for example if someone describes a sexual harassment incident and corporate policy requires you to act.

UNDERSTANDING YOUR ORGANIZATION'S CULTURAL THEMES

After several interviews, you may sense some common themes: the relationship between the bottom and top halves of the work culture; meanings attached to events in the organization or to relationships and communications. As you learn to listen for themes, you will build a picture in your mind of the cultural landscape. Work cultures are constantly evolving, and themes range from transient to deep underlying patterns.

A simple way for the management team to understand themes is to discuss their interviews. We said earlier that interviews are strictly confidential; you must never discuss whom you talked with, mention specific situations, or take an action based on what a particular person said. But it is essential to discuss

▶ **General areas people talk about.** ("In three of my interviews, people talked about their concerns with safety issues on our new delivery schedules.")

▶ **What people do not talk about.** ("While I gave everyone plenty of opportunity to talk about harassment, nobody picked up on it. I wonder if we might be thinking it is a bigger issue than it is?")

▶ **Feelings you had during interviews.** ("I felt tense. He was uncomfortable talking with me at first, but after 20 minutes he relaxed.")

Use a flip chart. Write down what people say. Look at the list and discuss it. As the cultural themes emerge, the managers will become more sensitive to what is on people's minds. This will affect how they handle everyday operational activities. This in turn will affect the work culture. Cultural changes will gradually show up in future interviews.

❖ **By revealing the organization's cultural themes, the interview directly develops the culture.**

THE "PARALLEL ORGANIZATION"

The "Parallel Organization" is a series of meetings where everyone in the organization can discuss and build understanding, relationships, openness, and trust. Work cultures are unbalanced, so by emphasizing the top half of the work culture, the parallel organization helps balance the culture.

Most organizations have operational meetings to share information and make decisions. Whether the business is sales, insurance, or widget making, production pressures usually make these meetings infertile soil for discussing human issues. Perhaps in some ideal land, the human and operational become one, but meanwhile operational meetings focus on information, analysis, and decision making, things that play little part in the human side. The human side requires other things to work well. Trust and openness are not handed down from above. They take time and caring.

Groups in the parallel organization usually meet once a month or weekly with the employee teams. The parallel organization is almost as effective as the interview for changing how top leaders behave, for developing the work culture. Four elements are:

▶ **Management Communications Meetings** of the top management team for planning and steering.

▶ **"Next Team" Meeting(s)** to involve other department managers and supervisors.

▶ **Employee Involvement Teams** such as Quality Circles—problem-solving teams of non-managers.

And if you have a union:

▶ **The Joint Labor-Management Committee** (JLMC). Monthly "nonagenda" meetings of the company and union leadership.

As you begin building the parallel organization some managers will say, "Why do we need more meetings? I'm too busy. Meetings don't get work done," which means "Can't we keep our work culture unbalanced? I don't want to face people (or myself). I joined management to treat people as objects." Be patient.

MANAGEMENT COMMUNICATIONS MEETINGS

The first step in developing the organization's culture and in building the parallel organization is holding top management meetings. This one-and-a-half to two-hour monthly meeting is usually over lunch, on-site. This is a "nonagenda" meeting, which means the subject is relationships, communications, experiences—the human side of work.

For most managers, these nonagenda meetings seem strange at first. Discussing relationships is unfamiliar and often uncomfortable. But after three or four meetings, as some important issues—often about territoriality, personal feelings, or interdepartmental situations—come out and nobody has a heart attack, the managers begin to look forward to the lunches.

Managers soon find these meetings to be so positive that they feel they have risen above the understanding of others in the operation. This is realistic because they are exploring the fourth level of the work culture, while the rest of the culture is dominated by the third level.

Meanwhile one or two managers may have started similar discussions in their departments. These may be separate nonagenda meetings or part of regular weekly meeting with time set aside to discuss relationships and communications.

☞ This is an evolutionary process. As the leader, direct that there will be meetings, certain people will attend, and the subject will be the human side of the work culture. The next step depends on where you are after the last step. Look for pockets of readiness and respond to them. Like evolution itself, the next step is usually a surprise—a good surprise.

After six to nine months, the group is often ready for a half-day meeting. Later they may decide to have an annual two-or three-day retreat where deep-seated issues come out safely for discussion

"NEXT TEAM" MEETINGS

As top management becomes more comfortable discussing human issues, it is time to draw managers from the next layer into a similar process.

These groups might cross department lines, be within one unit, or may include everyone of similar rank. Group size varies from three or four people to seventy or more. Very large groups do not allow much individual participation and can be chaotic unless very skillfully managed. The best size is between five and fifteen people.

☞ Because these "next team" meetings look only at the top half of the company culture, they are culturally uncomfortable. Top managers must encourage them if they are to take hold. That means asking supervisors who attend, "How are your meetings going?" and sharing personal experiences from your top management meetings.

At the early stages of this process, some managers and supervisors might say, "Why are we doing this? I have work to do. What are these for?" After two or three meetings, most will settle into sharing their experiences, although some may never become truly open. That is a natural part of diversity.

Typically each supervisor group meets once a month for one to one-and-a-half hours. In some organizations, a manager from the top group attends as a communication link to the top management meetings. In other companies, a supervisor from each "next team" will attend the manager's meeting. How you do it depends on the company culture, on trust and openness, and on work flow and logistical issues. There is no one best way. Work it out with those involved.

The new relationships improve operational meetings. Information flows more smoothly, work flow problems occur less often, and the satisfaction felt by managers and supervisors is contagious to employees below.

This sets the stage for the next piece of the parallel organization, the Employee Involvement Teams.

EMPLOYEE INVOLVEMENT TEAMS

An Employee Involvement Team (EIT) is a volunteer group of six to ten employees who meet once a week for an hour to identify, analyze, recommend, and act on a work-related issue of their choice.

Each EIT has a trained leader—usually a member of the team, often the work group's supervisor. In some companies, a manager attends each meeting in the role of facilitator.

An EIT steering committee, often the unit's full management group, designs and manages the involvement program. This committee meets monthly, keeps the program on track, reviews developments and hears EIT presentations. As members of both the EIT and the steering committee, facilitators smooth communications.

EITs begin after the steering committee develops the overall philosophy and schedule. Volunteer facilitators and leaders attend a short seminar by a consultant on EIT techniques and group leadership skills. They announce the program and invite employees to an orientation session. Those who choose to continue meet weekly as an EIT. Their first meetings are training sessions in problem solving, conducted by the facilitator and leader. After training, the team lists problems, issues, and opportunities, and selects one problem for detailed analysis. They present their recommendation to the steering committee, which has the power to approve.

The steering committee monitors each team's progress through the facilitator, through meeting minutes, and through discussion. When an EIT makes its final recommendation, there are no surprises. Normally the go ahead is immediate.

The most difficult problem the EIT leader (and facilitator) face is their new and unusual role. In their everyday role as manager or supervisor, they give instructions and answer questions. In an EIT, the members identify what problem to work on, how to analyze it, and what to recommend. The leader guides the process but does not direct the content.

Started in the U.S. in the 1970s, employee involvement teams, such as Quality Circles, were inspired by Japanese success stories. In typical American style, companies rushed in. Suddenly there were too many Quality Circles in a culture not ready for them, not enough control, many failures. Then companies changed the names and directed them more, for example by selecting the issue for the group to work on. Today we find many types of employee problem-solving and participation groups ranging from self-directed to those tightly controlled from above.

Most organizations can handle one EIT for every 100-150 people, although I once worked with an 80-person company that had two successful teams. One group is possible, two allow the leaders to discuss progress with each other and get support, three are better. Start small with two or three, adding another only when you sense the system is ready.

Organizational cultures do not encourage integrative systems thinking. Even though teams are set up to improve employee involvement, managers may forget and push teams to solve particular operating problems. Managers do not need to push. Employees, well aware of their work problems and the need to produce, are only too pleased to use the EIT to solve long-standing aggravations they experience on their job.

Meeting for one hour each week adds up to less than two weeks a year. Some topics I have seen:

► Write from scratch a 150-page laboratory test manual.

► Solve production line problems and reduce waste.

► Work with product suppliers to improve component quality.

► Put in place new structures and practices to better integrate the unit's work with other units.

Employee teams are usually so involving that people take work home, either in minds or folders. In one EIT, a member was on maternity leave. After her third week away she brought her newborn to the EIT meetings, returning home afterwards. That is commitment.

JOINT LABOR-MANAGEMENT COMMITTEE (JLMC)

If your organization has a union, the JLMC may be for you. It parallels and complements, but in no way replaces, the traditional bargaining relationship between labor and management.

The JLMC is a monthly one-and-a-half to two-hour meeting between the company and union leadership. It discusses communications, relationships, plans, and interpretations of work events. It excludes contractual issues, grievances, and other items discussed in normal labor-management meetings.

The JLMC is difficult to start; it takes courage on management's part. Even when both groups agree to get-together, initial meetings are often filled with suspicion and fear. Each group sees the other as an adversary: "Is this just another way to get an advantage in the negotiations? Will they use what we talk about here to my disadvantage in other meetings?"

Sometimes discussions begin with war stories, jokes about each organization's foibles, little victories, or pranks. As each party sees that the meetings stay away from contract issues, the other side does not misuse confidentialities, and everyday work issues outside of the JLMC are handled with greater sensitivity; people become more open, sharing new information.

For example, at one plant the union did not believe management's statistics. After six JLMC meetings, discussions moved to what lay behind the worker's compensation costs, which were crippling the company. Understanding and believing the seriousness of the issue for the first time, union leaders decided they would not tolerate their members abusing the system. Problems of excessive lost time disappeared immediately and permanently.

Discussing the people side of future plans is the main topic. Others are safety, diversity, favoritism, competition, Employee Involvement Teams, quality programs, and in seasoned JLMCs, the relationship between productivity and job security.

❖ **The JLMC is a place for the leaders of two traditionally adversarial groups to build relationships around human issues in the workplace.**

RETREATS

A retreat is a special time for a group to look at the human side of the job and of working together. Retreats range from a half-day get-together at a hotel to a week at a country lodge.

Preparation is important. Interview each other, create agenda items, involve others in developing topics and planning for managing the unit during your absence. Before you leave, know what will be discussed and what results you expect.

A three-day retreat seems to work well for many managers, perhaps leaving Saturday afternoon, arriving at the retreat site Saturday evening. This gives all day Sunday and Monday, leaving for home at noon on Tuesday, back at the office on Wednesday.

Because retreats focus on relationships and teamwork, they usually combine formal work sessions with recreation and social events. Arrange activities to include everyone—tennis, trail riding, hiking, swimming, fishing, golf. Nongolfers can play with borrowed clubs if the game is "best ball." The spirit should be cooperative, doing things together, not competitive. Fight your competitors in the marketplace, not your work associates. Work should be shelter from the competition of the marketplace, not an extension of it.

Some managers will be cooperative in meetings but combative at games. I recall one rigid, authoritarian supervisor getting even for his daytime frustrations with teamwork and cooperation by emptying everyone's pockets each night over poker.

Retreats are the only place where managers take enough time to look deeply into people's experiences and feelings about relationships and work events. What managers say and do together at a retreat can change how they work for years to come. Managers recall experiences at retreats as some of the most important in their career.

Cost-cutting efforts in American companies have affected retreats, often for the good. Low-priced condominiums with the team doing the cooking can be more fun and build teamwork faster and stronger than being catered to at a fancy resort.

THE LANDSCAPE METAPHOR

We are the children of our landscape. –Lawrence Durrell, *Justine*

Many important cultural issues about relationships, values, meanings, hopes, and fears are difficult, if not impossible to put into words. To make these more understandable, Meridian Group developed the "landscape metaphor." This is how to do it.

☞ The group's facilitator says, "Tell me some things you might see in a landscape." Write down what people say as single words. If the group gets onto one track, widen their view with "How about the tropics?" or "What other types of terrain do we have in America?"

ITEMS IN A LANDSCAPE		
mountains	trees	houses
sky	birds	people
ocean	ships	islands
roads	cars	freeways
deserts	oasis	animals
airplanes	valleys	cliffs
buildings	cities	parks
paths	schools	fields
sun clouds	moon	stars
children	home	family
competitors		islands

When the list seems well rounded say, "Now I would like you to take 40 minutes and as a group draw a picture of your organization using the landscape as a metaphor. We are not looking for artistry. The picture should include what is important to each of you. You have many experiences about work that you can describe this way. Discuss them, and agree on some general picture that will let everything be included. Everyone should contribute. Any questions? . . . When I return in 40 minutes I would like to hear how you decided to do this—your process—and from each of you I'd like a description of what the drawing means. Enjoy yourselves."

The first time a group does this they will find it very strange. Some may be embarrassed: "Adults don't do things like this." But the group soon gets into the swing of it.

If the group is eight or more, they should break into groups of four to six and do their drawings away from each other. Each group should be a mix of people with different jobs.

Creative metaphors result. Forests with tall trees, car races, mountain climbing, war ships at sea, battles, old galleons and buried treasure, freeways and interchanges, rivers, playgrounds, money bags, sunshine. All describe important parts of the work culture with meanings that could not be conveyed so accurately, simply, or richly by other means.

When you return, ask each group to describe the process and how they went about it before they dive into the details of what the drawing means. Then ask someone to describe the drawing. Have others talk about the pieces they contributed and their own meanings. Explanations, discussion and questions from others usually takes 10-15 minutes per drawing.

Drawing a cultural landscape together is a powerful experience. Memories of the metaphor, details of the drawing, and special meanings remain alive for the participants for many years.

☞ The content and process of the landscape make an excellent beginning for a retreat, allowing later discussion of material that otherwise would not surface. During the retreat, tape the drawings on the wall for later reference. The landscape drawing is typically of the current situation and issues, or the view down the road—a glimpse into the future.

These drawings are examples.

How you do it is as important as what you do.

The Decision Process

The daily process of making decisions—particularly *how* you make them—expresses organizational values and is one of the most powerful ways to create an engaging, humane, and open organizational culture. If you practice what is in this chapter, you can become skilled at leading effective group discussions and building consensus.

Do not try to do it all at once. Start with something you feel comfortable with. Gradually add new pieces.

THE LEADER'S ROLE—SUBSTANCE OR PROCESS?

In his memoirs, Napoleon tells this story: One evening, he sat outside his tent with his generals planning the next day's battle. While discussing a certain battalion, he glanced at a nearby hill. On waking the next morning, he looked up and saw the battalion on the hill. When he asked why it  was there, a general said, "Isn't that what you wanted, sir? You looked at the hill last evening as we discussed that battalion."

You can imagine how strong the field of authoritarianism was in Napoleon's day—"Little Napoleon" still means authoritarian. Small wonder Napoleon's generals scurried to please.

Most managers have experienced this. Employees are eager to satisfy the chief. We are all anxious to please Dad. Employees look for any signal that might suggest how the leader is feeling, what he or she might like. Many leaders are hesitant to give opinions because people hear them as directives.

To avoid this, separate your opinions from the decision process. Decisions have two parts:

▶ **What** is done—the substance, content, or opinions.

▶ **How** it is done—the decision process.

The more clearly you can separate the substance from the process, the more successful you will be as leader. Members often pull leaders to discuss substance. If you yield to that pull, you may lose control of the process.

You are the conductor; they are the orchestra. Together you can make fine music.

❖ **Set the cultural stage by leading the decision process to involve others in the substance.**

DECISIONS—AUTOCRATIC, CONSULTATIVE, OR GROUP?

No one way of making decisions works in every situation. Some decisions, like how to do a weld, do not require consensus. Other decisions, like scheduling vacations, would be a disaster without involvement. Most issues that rise to management's level are complex matters without simple solutions. To decide how to manage the decision process, look at the situation's context, the problem itself, and the values you want to convey.

There are three general ways to make a decision:

▶ **Autocratic.** You make the decision yourself. You may or may not ask others for information.

▶ **Consultative.** You get ideas from others and then make the decision yourself. It may or may not reflect their influence.

▶ **Group.** You discuss the problem as a group, leading toward a consensus. You might not even give your opinion.

You can evaluate decisions in four ways:

▶ **Quality.** Is it good technically?

▶ **Commitment.** Will people make it work?

▶ **Culture.** The effect of the decision process on the work culture. Did it improve people's attitudes, values and involvement? Did it pass the "bulletin board test"?

▶ **Time.** The amount of time required to make the decision. Did it pay off in improving the quality of the decision, the commitment of people, or the development of the work culture?

The values of an organization show through in how it involves people and groups in decisions that affect them. If decisions come down from on high, people feel differently than if their own thoughts are included in the process. If nobody appreciates people's ideas, creativity, and experience, they will probably stay uninvolved.

Fifteen years ago, many managers would bring in special *facilitators* to manage the decision-making process in meetings. These were usually from the personnel department, or they were outsiders. The message was clear: "This is not what real managers do."

Today many managers understand that managing the decision process is a key part of their job. They see their role in meetings as setting the stage for others to be productive. They hold together both the human and the operational, the top and the bottom of culture.

This does not mean abdicating responsibility or making every decision with the whole group. It just means involving people in the decisions that affect them.

Mature work groups often make decisions without any apparent group participation because there has been so much prior discussion about goals, values, and roles, and because people trust each other. Genuine understanding exists.

❖ **Whenever possible, use a decision process that involves the people affected by the decision.**

CONSENSUS

The quality of a decision depends largely on the process that leads to it, not on the final statement. The best decisions are those with input and commitment from the people affected. That takes a process of consensus that involves participation, openness, questioning, discussion, and persuasion.

Consensus emerges after all opinions are aired. Each participant must feel that they are heard and that their issues are considered. The process ends as the consensus becomes obvious and someone in the group announces it. At a minimum, this means that all members agree to support the decision even though they may not all agree with it.

☞ You do not have to do anything new, just do your everyday work with a human touch. A climate for consensus grows as people become aware that you value their participation, creativity, and competence.

Consensus takes more time than other processes, but that time is more than made up by the ease and speed of carrying out consensus decisions. If you have a solution in mind, you can use consensus to decide how to do it.

Some differences between the old adversarial process and a consensus process:

Adversarial process	Consensus process
Us versus them	We, together
Focus on differences	See differences but focus on commonalities
Democratic voting (win-lose)	Discussion and understanding (win-win)
Start with answers and positions	Start with problems, values, and meanings
Give or take ground (control power)	Establish common ground (persuasion)
Directive	Participative
In a context of power and authority (hierarchy)	In a context of greater equality

TIPS FOR BUILDING A CONSENSUS

If you are a group leader and want consensus on an issue, try these tips. You can use them in a meeting, and many can be used in one-on-one discussions. They help people focus on common ground and avoid conflict.

- ▶ **Accept** all comments at face value. Assume no hidden meanings. Be simple, act in good faith, avoid judging or expressing your opinion.

- ▶ **If members want to pass authority to you,** pass it back to the group. Hold the group accountable for its actions. Ask the group to handle its own internal scraps. If someone asks you a question on the subject being discussed, turn the question back to the group: "Would someone like to answer that question?" Then remain silent.

- ▶ **Give information,** if you are the only person who has information on the topic. Information is different from opinion.

- ▶ **Ask the group how it is progressing toward goals.** Remind the group of the agreed upon ground rules. Your initial task as a leader is to help the group agree on rules for managing itself.

- ▶ **Teamwork.** Ask those who do not follow the rules but want to stay in the group to decide if that is reasonable.

- ▶ **Turn talk about outsiders back** into the group. If people talk about "them out there" suggest that they work on things they can control, things that are their responsibility.

- ▶ **The answer is theirs.** Do not imply that there is one best way, a hidden answer known only to you or to management.

- ▶ **Ask for suggestions** from the group as a whole rather than from one person.

- ▶ **Check** whether a suggestion offered by someone is acceptable to the person who voiced the concern or question: "Did that answer your question?"

- ▶ **Encourage** someone to voice a tentative or incomplete idea. Wait silently for someone to get their thoughts together.

► **Intervene** when members disagree or object to each other's ideas: "Before we start judging ideas, let's first hear from everyone on how they see our office relationships (the subject at hand). We can evaluate later, O.K.?"

► **Probe** to see if there is a suggestion or concern behind someone's questions: "Say some more about that." "What were you thinking of?" "Did you have an idea of what we could do with that?" "Why?"

► **Understand**. If someone is rambling, ask them to connect back with the subject: "And tell us how that connects to our office relationships?".

► **Postpone**. Ask someone to hold off introducing a new topic until you have finished the current one: "That is a good point. Can we first finish with the one we are on and then get back to that?" You might write the idea on a separate "Issue Bin" sheet.

THE FOUR-STEP DECISION-MAKING PROCESS

A good consensus process follows the basic steps of decision making. I like the simplicity and ease of this four-step model. If your organization is comfortable with another model, use it. Whatever model you choose, use it.

1. Describe the **situation** clearly.

2. List possible **alternative** actions.

3. Agree on the **selection criteria**—what is important when choosing between alternative actions.

4. Agree on **actions**, who will do what.

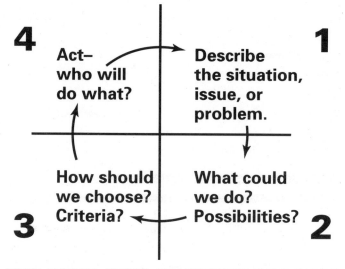

THE FOUR STEP DECISION PROCESS

As the team's leader you have brought the key players into one room. You have agreed on ground rules and agreed to use the four-step decision process (which you taped on the wall as a reminder). You have agreed on the topic. As facilitator you will lead the group through the decision-making process, helping them to supply the substance. Here is what to do.

1. WHAT IS THE SITUATION, ISSUE, PROBLEM?

☞ At the top of the sheet, state the topic. Under that write "Situation—issues, problem." Say that "'Situation' means just that: the context, the whole thing, all levels." "Situation" is broader than "problem," the analytic. Go around the group, in order, one person at a time. Ask for one thing they experience about the situation that concerns them personally, or that they feel is important. Write what they say on the pad, numbering items. Go around the group until no one has anything to add. Allow one statement per person. Do not allow discussion or evaluation.

If someone wants to challenge a point, for example: "I don't think that's true (or, a problem)," you say, "I understand you may not necessarily agree with how each person sees the situation, but right now we only want a complete listing of how we each see it. We will discuss and evaluate items later. O.K.?" Tear off the sheets, numbering each one, and tape them to the wall.

When the list seems complete, seek agreement. If you do not, some people will be unable to move to the next step. Agreement at each step is fundamental to building consensus. "Do we all agree that this is the full situation as we see it? Anything more?" Take your time with the silence. A full description includes items from all five levels of logical types, page 52.

OUR OFFICE RELATIONSHIPS ①
1. Situation—Issues, problems

1. Not enough information from above about what's happening.
2. Sometimes there is too much work and I can't get help.
3. We don't get the production numbers until late on Friday.
4. I don't know what others are doing, how can I help them?
5. Why don't we have flexible start times?

2. WHAT COULD WE DO?

☞ Use the same procedure you used for step 1. Write "What could we do?" or "Possibilities" at the top of the new sheet. Then say, "Let's go around the group again. Feel free to say anything that comes to your mind as a possible action. Use your imagination. Items may connect to issues on the first list but they do not have to. They may just be things you would like to see done. We want as long a list as we can get. Be creative—anything goes!" Again, allow no discussion or evaluation.

When the group has no more ideas, seek agreement. "Are you sure there is nothing else you would like to see done?" Silence. . . "Do we agree that we now have a complete description of the problem and all the possibilities as far as we see it? . . . Good, we are half way through the decision."

OUR OFFICE RELATIONSHIPS ④

2. What could we do? Possibilities?

1. Hire a new clerk.
2. Set up a short term task team with Production on numbers.
3. Talk to HR about what other plants are doing with flexible start times.
4. Rethink how we allocate work in the department.
5. Meet weekly on these issues.

3. HOW SHOULD WE CHOOSE?

☞ Label this new sheet "3. How should we choose—Criteria?" Then say, "What is important to keep in mind when we look over the 'Possibilities' and 'Problem' pages? How should we select from all the possibilities? What are the criteria?" If someone speaks in favor of an item on the "Possibilities" list, you might say, "What we need to know is why you think that's important, what are your criteria?"

You will get items such as cost, timing, regulations, technical feasibility, and office politics. This step may be difficult for some people. Allow plenty of silence while they think.

OUR OFFICE RELATIONSHIPS ⑦
3. How should we choose—Criteria?

1. Cost
2. Technical Issues
3. Is it in line with company policy?
4. Is it in line with our annual plan?
5. Environmental Issues?
6. Can we do it in-house?
7. Effect on other company plants?
8. How long will it take?
9. Do we need 100% approval?

At this point someone will probably suggest voting on, or grouping, items from the "Issues" or "Possibilities" lists. If no one does, then you suggest it: "Now that we know what is important in choosing, let's look back at the "Possibilities" list. Take a piece of paper and write down the numbers of the four items that are most important to you personally. We are not going to make a decision yet; this vote is to understand what the group feels is important." Tally the votes and mark the top items from the "Possibilities" list.

4. WHO WILL DO WHAT?

☞ After steps 1, 2, and 3, you should feel comfortable saying, "Now we all understand the issues, the possibilities, and the criteria. You have voted and know what is important to the group. We are three quarters finished with the decision." Point to the four-step decision circle on the wall.

There may now be a consensus. Test for this: "Is there a solution or mix of solutions here that seems to fit?" If nothing comes, try, "Can anyone suggest what we should do now?" Be silent; wait. If there is still no response, you might ask, "Are any of the actions in anyone's area? Does anyone want to take some items from the list?" As they volunteer, write their initials against the items on the "Possibilities" list, or start a new "Actions" list. Often two or more people will take the same item. Allow plenty of time for this step.

(Mature groups take responsibility for their own problems and solutions. The group should not come up with a solution for someone else, or for a group that is not in the room. If another group or person's input is obviously needed, your group may meet with them later or invite them to the next meeting.)

☞ When they have put their names against enough items, say, "To make sure we keep the ball rolling on this, when should we meet again? How about after you have contacted anyone else who should be involved and had a chance to think about next steps? When would that be?" Usually several days or a week is enough.

Once they agree, say, "Then we will meet on (date and time). Can you all be here then? . . . Please talk this over with others who were not here today and sort out any items that involve several of you. Any questions? . . . We did a lot today. Good job. Thank you all."

The newsprint pages can be photocopied down to regular page size and distributed as minutes. These handwritten pages are far more effective than typed minutes.

USING THE DECISION PROCESS TO REORGANIZE

Using consensus, experienced organizations can handle big changes.

John, the executive director of an 800-person government regulatory agency, telephoned. John and I had worked together for three years. He and his management group had become a smoothly functioning team, understanding and using the four-step decision process. The agency faced an immediate and complete restructuring, and John was concerned that this would cause such disruption and anger that the agency might cease to function.

Over lunch, I suggested John use the reorganization as an opportunity to involve everyone and the four-step process to do it. "Begin by stating the situation clearly. Tell everyone that in four weeks the agency will be reorganized with everyone in new roles and you will use the following steps to get there, making sure everyone lands where they want to be.

"In the first week, each department manager will meet with his or her people, outlining the task and the decision process. Each supervisor will do the same. At these meetings, employees will discuss the situation, what they would like to see considered during the reorganization, and other issues they want to bring to management's attention. The managers will summarize these meetings, bringing their findings to a meeting of department heads.

"In the second week, the management committee will discuss each department's issues, come up with a consensus, and respond to each department. After that meeting, the supervisors will ask their people to list possibilities, describe what role they want to play in the reorganized agency. The supervisors will bring this back to the management group.

"In the third week, consider what is important when finalizing the decision. Everyone should now understand the issues, possibilities, and criteria. Supervisors will inform their managers, who will get-together and once again provide feedback. One more round and everybody's new jobs should be settled."

John thought this sounded workable. I wished him luck, inviting him to call me if he needed help. I heard nothing.

Three months later, John and I had lunch again. He said they completed the reorganization in three weeks rather than four, and disruption and complaints were negligible.

LEADING BY ASKING QUESTIONS

As a group leader or member, you should try to create the kind of meetings that you personally enjoy. Do you like your ideas and experiences pulled into the discussion? Do you like appreciation and solving your own problems? A good way to create this experience for others is by asking questions—of your boss, peers, or subordinates, anytime, anyplace.

Questions make you listen, building teamwork, involvement, and commitment. These questions work well person-to-person or in a group. They connect to the four-step decision process.

Step 1 — How do we see the situation or issue?

How do you personally experience the situation?
Can you give me an example?
What are the facts and issues here?
What really is the problem?
(Silence. Let them talk; you listen.)

Step 2 — What could we do?

What do you think we could do?
What would you personally like to see happen?
What are other possibilities?
Let's brainstorm this one. What ideas do you have?
Any wild, way-out, off-the-wall ideas?

Step 3 — How should we choose?

What should we keep in mind when we think about the "Possibilities" list?
How should we judge the ideas?
What are the constraints on this?
How about costs and timing?
Should we consult anybody else?

Step 4 — Who will do what?

Who wants to pick up on this one?
What should we do now?
What is our (your) next step?
When can you get back to me with your progress on this?

PERSONALITY AND DECISION MAKING

Our personality influences how we approach problems. We focus on those parts of decision making that are important and interesting to us. We each have different interests or strengths and use these in deciding. For a naturalist, these strengths may be in observing. A manager may want to apply ideas in the workplace. A statistician may emphasize theory. A mechanic may place high value on concrete, current experiences.

Conflicts and misunderstandings in groups often come from personal differences in how people approach decisions. For example, someone who feels we should collect all the information we can, carefully doing it right the first time, might be unhappy with someone who says, "Let's get on with this now. We can iron out any wrinkles later on."

You have probably been in meetings where people have said the following things. They are grouped by the four steps of the decision process. Remember that they reflect people's personalities resonating to the work culture.

1. **Situation**
    "What actually happened?"
    "Is that practical?"
    "It worked last time."

2. **Possibilities**
    "Do we have all the facts?"
    "Think before leaping."
    "Let's do it right."

3. **Criteria—evaluation**
    "It should work like this."
    "I don't care if it doesn't work yet."
    "What's the principle behind this?"
    "We already tried that and it didn't work"

4. **Act**
    "Let's get on with it."
    "We'll fix any problems later."
    "Let's stop talking about it."

A person with a high need for control will often try to influence the group to his or her preferred area (usually the action area). Because most work cultures encourage authoritarianism, leaders often push for action, sometimes before the group is ready.

Just because a controlling leader says, "Let's move on this now," and you think this must be O.K., it does not mean that it is the right thing to do. But it is difficult in autocratic work cultures to question authority by saying, "Before we act on this, are we sure we have heard everyone's concerns and ideas?"

A healthy decision process balances action with each of the other steps in the decision process, and, when time allows, involves everyone affected by the decision.

❖ **As a leader, be careful that your own preferences for certain parts of the decision process do not unduly sway the group.**

BRAINSTORMING

Brainstorming stimulates new ideas. Use it to learn what members think about problems, or solutions, or what to do next, or anything else about the group's work. In brainstorming:

▶ Quickly come up with as many ideas as possible—quantity, not quality, is the key.

▶ Do not allow evaluative comments.

Here's how:

☞ At the top of the pad, write down the subject as clearly as you can. For example, "Issues in our office?" is better than just "Problems?"

Ask each member in rotation for one idea. Continue until you have written down all ideas. If a person has no ideas, they can simply say, "Pass."

Write each idea exactly as the person said it, numbering each one. If you have to abbreviate a long idea, ask, "Did I get that down right?" Do not judge any idea as stupid; sometimes the craziest ideas have the seeds of the most creative solutions.

Number each page, tear it off, and tape it to the wall. Make no comments about any idea. Don't even say, "Good idea" or "I like that." You can say something neutral such as, "Thank you" or "Next." If someone makes an evaluative or critical comment, say, "Please hold your comments until we get to the evaluation step."

If an issue or idea is not on the current topic you might put it on a separate page called "Issue Bin."

Laughter and informality encourage creativity and new ideas. Exaggeration or the use of metaphor also helps. "If this were an animal, what kind of animal would it be?" or "Forget the cost" or "If this were a landscape, or a picture, or a Greek myth, what would it look like?"

If people have time to think about the subject well in advance, they will have more ideas.

GROUPING IDEAS

The team will often want to consolidate long lists, putting similar ideas together.

☞ To group ideas, circle the first numbered item on the list and ask, "What other items should be circled, what other numbers go with this one?" Take your time, let them think. When you have finished circling related items, draw a square around the next item on the list that is not circled (it might be item 2 or 3.) Continue, using triangles, semi-circles, or colors.

When you have grouped every item (and a group with one is O.K.) go back to the first circled set and ask, "What will we name this group? Are there some words that I could underline to define this group?" (Usually two to four words will be enough.) Repeat this with each of the groups.

RANKING IDEAS—VOTING

Voting can help a group learn what is important to the whole group.

Whether they will admit it to themselves or to others, many people are unable to speak their mind in groups. They may be intimidated by the group as a whole or by some high ranking or forceful person. We all want to be part of the team. Speaking up may separate us. Whether real or imagined, the fear of repercussion is easy to overcome. To learn what people really think, use secret voting. Do this informally.

☞ Tear up a sheet of paper and give each person a small piece. Say, "Write the number of the three (or four if the list is very long) items that are most interesting to you personally, that you would actively support. I will tally your votes. This is not a vote to decide what to do, but a vote to give you information about how we all feel about the issues." After the tally, say, "Now you know which items are the most interesting to the team as a whole."

When you suggest secret voting, often an authoritarian, showing exaggerated nonchalance, will say, "I don't see why we should do that. I'm not afraid to say what I think." Do not respond, or do so mildly: "Well Bill, perhaps not everyone feels the way you do. This won't take long. O.K.?" Tear up the sheet of paper and hand out the pieces. Groups soon get used to secret voting. Some use it routinely.

USING SILENCE TO MANAGE

We tend to fill empty spaces (dark forests, abandoned old houses, etc.) with imaginary scenes, some of which are scary and make us anxious. Silence is an empty space. To avoid anxiety, we fill silence with talk. To our primitive unconscious, meetings and work groups are very scary places. In groups, most people are anxious. That is why silence is rare in a formal meeting. To our unconscious, silence is just too dangerous.

Closer to the conscious and less profound level, the anxiety might have other causes:

► The group leader might be afraid to lose control. "If there is silence, someone else might step in and take over and I will be done for."

► "If I'm silent, one of my peers might step in (and appear better than me), so I must speak."

► "People might think I'm dumb if I don't answer immediately, so I can't be silent."

Groups as a whole behave much less maturely than the individuals within them are capable of behaving. Groups often rush to fill the void of silence rather than face what is actually happening—the fear—inside the group. "Group think" is a common name for the decisions made by groups that hurry quickly to action, often following the leader like lemmings. A skillful leader uses silence to help the group get in touch with what is happening and discover where it should go, rather than allowing it to mindlessly act. To help a group get in touch with itself, try these.

☞ At the start of a meeting say, "Work life is busy and there often isn't time to think quietly about a subject. Let us take five minutes before we start the meeting and think about our office relationships (your subject), what it means to you, how it fits into your daily work, what you might like to do about it, and what you would like to see happen in this meeting."

During a problem discussion, say, "Let's just take a few minutes and not talk. We're looking at some possible things we could do. Take a piece of paper and write down three alternative actions you think are possible. After we have all done that, let's go around the group and hear all the ideas." Have them say only one idea each. You may have to go around the group three times. "Pass" is O.K.

If someone asks you a question, but you want the group involved, look at the asker and nod your head to signal understanding. Look around the group, silently inviting someone else to respond. Say nothing.

RESPONDING TO HOSTILE QUESTIONS

Most hostility comes from outside the group—from home or from a past experience with authority. Hostility is a way people express their frustrations. Do not take hostility personally, and do not act defensively.

☞ As a leader, your role is to maintain a productive environment. Hostility gets in the way of work. Stay in your role. Do not escalate. Do not join the battle. Try to demonstrate the type of behavior you would like to see in others. Set a powerful stage, one that encourages everyone's involvement.

There are several ways to respond to hostility. Some are productive and some are not. You can:

► **Fight directly,** escalate, join the battle.

► **Fight indirectly,** wait until later and shove. "Don't get mad, get even."

► **Withdraw,** check out emotionally, back off, stop talking.

► **Hold even,** do not argue, but restate your position.

► **Postpone,** "Let's discuss that later"—not avoiding but putting it off.

► **Dialogue,** exchange information, understand what led to each other's views, communicate, look for common ground.

As a cultural leader, behave in a way that shows openness and understanding, invites participation, and leads to solving the problem. If someone attacks you, recognize the attacker's feelings but don't escalate the fight. Stay in your role and keep communications open. "Say some more about that," or "Can you give me an example of something that happened to you recently like that?" or "Thank you. That's is an interesting point. Does anyone else have something to add?" Pick up your coffee, take a sip, and look around the room, establishing eye contact to invite reaction.

Write down what they say and look around the group: "Anything else?" or "Have you any thoughts on what might be done about this?" or "Is there something you would like me to do with this?"

If the complaint is about some other group's actions, you might say, "I'd like you to get-together with them and talk this over. If we can help that happen for you, let us know. If you try that and you still disagree, let us know. Please let us know what you decide to do."

Avoid statements such as, "There's nothing we can do about that here." Do not use your authority to win, to close out communications. That only shows rigidity and defensiveness. You do not want those qualities in your organization, so do not model them.

PASSIVE AGGRESSIVE SILENCE

Have you ever conducted a meeting, asked for ideas, and met with silence? Members may be thinking, "They already know what I think." or "My point isn't important." or "She will do what she wants to do anyway."

Whatever the reason, silence frustrates a leader. She senses that the group is attacking her and feels defenseless against it.

If you are the leader of a quiet group, try these.

▶ Ask a direct question of the group, or of a member, or go around the group, one at a time, asking for ideas.

▶ Establish ground rules. State the purpose of the meeting. Let people know what they should do, what their role is, that you want their input. Use the four-step decision process.

▶ Ask the group for help. "We seem to be very quiet today. That makes me nervous. Can someone help me please?"

▶ Remind them that your job is to get participation, that you need their help, that you want their input.

▶ If you feel up to it, discuss the silence with the group. They may be insecure, intimidated, fear the leader, the system, or peers. Be careful, you may be skating on thin ice.

If you are a member of a silent group:

▶ Ask directly, "Where are we?"

▶ Use a question. Do not make a statement.

▶ To get things back on track, ask what the subject is.

▶ Speaking up takes trust and a feeling of security. There may be reasons why members feel insecure—intimidation at work, fear of the leader, fear of the system, or fear of peers. Talking about your own fears or concerns might encourage others.

What people do comes mostly from the setting. Silence tells you about the work culture and about you as a leader. As a leader, manage the setting. Get expectations clear ahead of time, carefully select the participants, ask the group for help.

GROUP CODE OF CONDUCT

Most groups develop an informal set of rules that reflect the group's values. They let everybody know "How we do things here." Most groups seem to develop between five and fifteen items.

These rules come from some groups I have worked with.

- ▶ Listen to and show respect for the views of other members.
- ▶ Make others feel a part of the group.
- ▶ Criticize ideas, not people.
- ▶ Be open to, and encourage the ideas of others.
- ▶ We are each responsible for the team's progress.
- ▶ We are all equal during meetings.
- ▶ Follow the golden rule.
- ▶ The only bad question or suggestion is the one we do not hear.
- ▶ Be friendly.
- ▶ Try for win-win situations.
- ▶ Encourage and praise others, no sarcasm or criticism.
- ▶ Do not give solutions before everyone understands the problem.
- ▶ If someone will be affected by a decision, involve them.
- ▶ Attend all meetings and be on time.
- ▶ Carry out assignments on schedule.
- ▶ We will agree on and use a clear decision process.

☞ To develop your own list, go around the group asking for one item each. "Think about meetings that you have been in that were satisfying. What made them work well?" Have the group consolidate the list and agree on it. Rewrite it neatly and post it on the wall. If someone starts ignoring the rules, just point to the sheet and say, "Do we want to reconsider our agreement?"

EVALUATING MEETINGS

With the group

The "Plus/Delta" is a good way a group can quickly evaluate a meeting. It helps everyone understand what other people value, improves meetings, and is brief.

☞ Draw a vertical line down the center of the easel pad. At the top of the left column put + (plus sign). At the top of the right column put Δ (Delta). In engineer language, Delta means gap. As meeting leader, say, "Delta is the difference between what we did today and what we might do next time. It does not mean "problems." I'd like to hear the pluses, what you liked about this meeting, and the deltas, things we should change for the next meeting."

HOW WAS THE MEETING?	
+	Δ
Liked free discussion.	Should start on time.
Good ideas. Clear agenda.	Sometimes we rambled.
We finished on time.	Let's get data before the meeting.
Next step is clear.	
Good facilitation.	Invite marketing. A few zingers.

Go around the group, asking each person for one item for each column. Again, it is O.K. to "pass."

By yourself

Though few managers take formal time to do this, you might think about how you were as a facilitative leader, how you led the process.

▶ Did you feel good about the meeting? Were you satisfied?

- ▶ Did you notify the right people early enough about the time, place, and purpose of the meeting?

- ▶ Was the atmosphere informal, relaxed?

- ▶ Did all people participate? Did some dominate? Did some not speak? Did members listen to each other?

- ▶ Was there sarcasm, zingers, put-downs, etc.?

- ▶ Did people express disagreement courteously and with respect?

- ▶ Did you use silence well?

- ▶ Did you stay in role as facilitator? Did you focus on the process instead of the content?

- ▶ Did the meeting begin and end on time?

- ▶ Did you clean up the room for the next group?

If you know where you are going,
it doesn't matter where you start.

7

Regular Activities

Ow we manage regular activities makes all the difference. Developing a company's culture starts with a commitment but not a detailed master plan. It begins by paying careful attention to people in your daily actions. Each example in this chapter shows how the manager took a regular activity and placed people first.

Several of the examples are about boundary management. All systems must manage their boundaries. If our body did not maintain a careful boundary, with skin and blood, hostile organisms would soon invade. It is the same with organizations; you have to watch the door. Who we let into the organization and who we promote from one level to another are both parts of boundary management. Our values are demonstrated in our boundary management practices. The examples:

► Promoting.

► Hiring.

► Upward appraisal.

► Ranking managers for pay raises and bonuses.

► Managing the production process.

These represent only a few ways; there are many ways to approach any operational problem when you have people in mind.

❖ **There are many paths to an engaging and open work culture.**
(general systems maxim)

PROMOTING

Chuck, the maintenance manager in a unionized 300-person continuous process plant, had participated in company culture development efforts for two years. Sensitive to the need for involvement, he decided to try a new approach to selecting a mechanic for promotion to supervisor. He used the promotion process to build relationships.

He asked his clients, the production department, for their involvement. Ray, the production manager, and his supervisors developed selection criteria. Ray insisted that the supervisors not discuss individual candidates until they agreed on criteria.

Traditionally, the promotion went to the most proficient mechanic. But production supervisors rated technical excellence well below problem solving, communications and relationships, and ability to quickly mobilize people at the problem site.

Though their priorities surprised Chuck, he approved their criteria and gave them back to production, along with the candidates' names. Individually the production supervisors scored each candidate against the criteria and tallied their scores. The result was the first woman maintenance supervisor in the plant. She proved to be excellent.

This process:

► Involved those affected—the production supervisors.

► Exposed the promotion process to public scrutiny (the criteria were publicized). This demonstrated to the whole plant a new level of objectivity and openness. (Before this, mechanics believed it was all favoritism. "They promote those who suck up.")

► Showed production supervisors that they were valued in new ways.

► Built a bridge between two departments (Maintenance and Production) that had traditionally seen each other as adversaries.

► Produced a better operational decision.

HIRING

Eighteen months later, Chuck needed to hire five additional mechanics for his 70-person department. He decided to use the hiring process as an opportunity to involve people in new ways. With the cooperation of the maintenance supervisors and the plant management team, he asked his mechanics to form a hiring group. Six mechanics volunteered.

Chuck described his expectations and their roles. The mechanics met with the Human Resources Department to learn about hiring policy and procedures. Because the group had only a few hours a week to spend on the project, these early steps took two months. The mechanics developed a hiring process, which Chuck approved. They placed the newspaper advertisement, and, using criteria they developed, reduced the applicant list from several hundred to about forty.

After careful interviewing, using a predetermined format and questions, they cut the list down to six people. They presented Chuck with a convincing case for hiring all six. Chuck agreed. All six accepted the job offers.

Several months later, Chuck said, "The mechanics developed a more rigorous hiring process than we had used before. Now they are working very closely with the new hires to make sure that everyone succeeds. This process succeeded beyond anything I imagined. It was much better than I could have done, even if I had the time, which I didn't."

This process:

▶ Involved those affected—the other mechanics.

▶ Showed mechanics they were valued in new ways.

▶ Developed a new experience of competency in the hiring team members.

▶ Demonstrated to the whole plant a new level of involvement.

▶ Produced a higher quality operational result, including guaranteeing on-the-job success of the new hires.

▶ Made Chuck happy.

UPWARD APPRAISAL

In a major international corporation, a companywide survey revealed that managers did not listen and did not encourage participation. Upper management asked lower level managers to get feedback on their performance from subordinates.

Asking subordinates to criticize their bosses can be a ticklish situation, resulting in rancor and resentment or in nothing if employees lack the trust to speak up. George, an upper-middle-level manager in a 2,000-person plant, had participated for three years in work culture development efforts. He decided to hold a formal upward appraisal process with the 20 employees he directly supervised. George saw the upward appraisal as another opportunity to advance the human side.

For over a year, he had held two weekly meetings with his team. One was a traditional information sharing and decision-making meeting on operational issues. The other was an open-agenda meeting discussing communications, relationships, new ideas, and team problem solving.

At one of these second meetings, George outlined the upward appraisal, asking his team to decide all the details. George's subordinates used the same categories that George's superior used to evaluate him. These included communication, leadership, teamwork, creativity and innovation, planning and organizing, job knowledge, problem solving, and quality improvement.

The supervisors met without George to discuss each category. They agreed that George's behavior was not a one-sided thing: "It takes two to tango." To make any effective changes would require the cooperation of both George and his supervisors. They ranked the categories by "Which were most important to the group, which ones we want to work on with George over the next few months." They talked over how they wanted to work with George; then invited him into the room.

The ensuing hour-long discussion was exciting and productive. George pinned the worksheets on his office wall to demonstrate his commitment and to remind him of his half of the agreement.

Six months later, George and the group held a three-hour follow-up meeting, using a similar process.

This upward appraisal process:

▶ Involved those affected—the subordinates and George.

▶ Demonstrated to subordinates that managers valued feedback.

▶ Demonstrated to subordinates a new level of openness about a very sensitive area. This encouraged some to do a similar process with their own people.

▶ Encouraged George's peers to use a similar process.

▶ Was exciting for George and helped him develop his skills.

▶ Improved George's relationships and increased his respect by his people.

▶ Gave George specific feedback on his behavior which he could then work on with his people.

RANKING MANAGERS FOR PAY RAISES AND BONUSES

Very few companies have a satisfying process for ranking groups of managers and supervisors for pay raises and bonuses.

Ron, a senior manager in a 1,500-person continuous process chemical plant, had 100 subordinates in seven pay levels. A sensitive and humane manager, Ron decided not to use the company's traditional one-on-one, top-down ranking process. He would use a new process to involve people in new ways.

With the assistance of a facilitator, he called an all-day meeting to rank the people in his department for raises and bonuses. Managers and supervisors from pay grades one through six were in the room to discuss and rank the absent seventh level supervisors.

They discussed the first person on the seventh level list using pre-determined criteria. Then the facilitator said, "If this page had all of the seventh level people, would he be high, in the middle, or low?" The group placed the name in the middle of the page.

They then discussed the next person. The facilitator said, "Would this person be above or below the first?" Then, "And close to or far away from?" This process continued until all the seventh level people's initials were on the sheet.

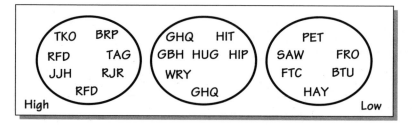

The next step was to draw a ring around like clusters of initials. By chance, the names clustered into obvious groups.

After much discussion, they assigned bonuses to each cluster.

Then the sixth-level people left the room and the fifth through first-level people used the same process to rank the sixth-level. The process continued until only the first-level group remained.

▶ While the process did not directly involve the people in their own ranking (this was partly done in a separate one-on-one process before the meeting), it let everyone in the room share in a fair process. To those below, upper management decisions all too often seem naïve, insensitive, or irrational, which discourages people from bringing more of themselves to work. This ranking process passed the "bulletin board test."* Everyone left the room confident that their own ranking would be fair.

▶ The process demonstrated to others in that plant (and, as it later turned out, in other plants) a new level of involvement and openness about a very sensitive and important subject close to everyone's heart and paycheck.

▶ The discussions made it clear to everyone present what qualities were looked for and what were seen as undesirable. The process joined words (what we say we want from managers) and actions (what we actually reward) together in a powerful way.

❖ **Every major decision should pass the bulletin board test.**

---

* The "bulletin board" test means, "Does the process or decision seem legitimate to others in the organization? If you put what you did on the bulletin board, would people approve or disapprove?" This is a good question for any manager or leader to ask prior to a decision.

MANAGING THE PRODUCTION PROCESS

The facility was a 250-person unionized Midwestern manufacturing plant with traditional, adversarial relationships among departments. A corporate vice president encouraged the plant manager to "try something new." Curt, a production supervisor, decided the atmosphere was ready for him to do what he had wanted to do for years—build better relationships inside his department.

Curt laid the groundwork with thank-you notes, interviews, and "management by walking around." He suffered the usual negative comments from peers, some subordinates, and at times from his immediate manager. "You are wasting time" he was told, and "not focusing on important things." He was even called "weak."

Meanwhile the plant manager was sowing other seeds, encouraging others. A change in the maintenance department brought Sal, a new maintenance supervisor, into Curt's production area. Sal and Curt saw that they could use the traditional morning production scheduling meetings to involve maintenance and production foremen more in decisions. They began by asking more questions. At first, the mechanics and production workers resisted. They were used to being told what to do. They were suspicious, perhaps thinking that volunteering information or opinions invited later reprisals or looked like apple polishing.

Over nine months, the climate gradually changed. Mechanics and production leads were making more and better decisions about the day's work and priorities. Before, these decisions were made by supervisors. Costs were dropping as high priority items were easily identified and getting quicker and better attention.

A visit to the plant by other plant managers created an opportunity for Curt and Sal to showcase their new participative process. They invited the visiting high level managers to the morning meeting of 20 mechanics, operators, foremen, engineer, and mid-manager. The engineer reviewed the previous day's production numbers and the new day's production plan. Lead foremen listed new mechanical problems, and mechanics updated the repair list from the previous day. Priorities were established and everyone left knowing what to do. The meeting took 20-30 minutes. Two visiting managers were so impressed they immediately implemented similar processes at their own plants.

Curt and Sal pushed forward, developing new procedures to expand and more deeply involve production and maintenance workers in decisions. They saw that the extra time taken in these meetings was more than offset by eventual savings. Understanding the big picture, mechanics scheduled their time better and required much less supervision. Production leaders now understood the mechanic's problems and limitations. Relationships between these traditional foes improved dramatically.

Two years later, costs were lower than in any other plant in the system. Other departments had adopted similar processes.

This process:

► Involved everyone in the production area.

► Demonstrated to subordinates that managers valued their expertise.

► Exposed the daily decision process to public scrutiny, demonstrating a new level of openness.

► Built a bridge between two departments (Maintenance and Production) that had seen each other as adversaries.

► Produced better operational decisions.

SUMMARY OF SECTION TWO

► The purpose of any culture is to serve the people in it, not vice-versa.

► Developing the work culture means starting with the people as the subject, not the object.

► If human values are the company's highest priority then productivity and profits will naturally flow.

► The most effective way of developing the work culture is to get to know people better using the "interview."

► Understanding your organization's cultural themes is fundamental to developing the culture.

► The "parallel organization" is an effective structure to develop the culture. The elements are:

> Management communications meetings
> "Next team" meetings
> Employee involvement teams
> The Joint Labor Management Committee

► *How* you make decisions—the decision process—is a key in developing the work culture.

► Decisions should involve those affected.

► Consensus decisions are the most powerful.

► There are an infinite number of ways to approach a situation if you start with people first. Some examples given were:

> Managing meetings
> Promoting
> Hiring
> Appraisals
> Pay raises and bonuses
> Production process

Reflections

In 1954, I took my first corporate job—summer employment as a salesperson in a chain store. Writing this book has made me reflect on these 40 years as employee, employer, manager, owner, teacher, and consultant. In this section, I will share some thoughts and conclusions.

Chapter 8—Why is culture change so hard? Some organizations slam the door on developing an engaging work culture. We will look at resistance, arrested cultural development, and fear, and suggest actions you might take to test your organization's cultural waters. We will also discuss using outside help in a culture development effort.

Chapter 9—The ideal, a person-centered work culture: The human values that managers need in order to develop an engaging company culture. As cultural leaders, managers must look at themselves, at fundamental American values, and at their people.

The closing pages explore work cultures that welcome change.

section three

You can't get there from here!
　　　　　—farmer's wise directions

Why Is Culture Change So Hard?

Fifteen years ago my partner and I worked with a marketing group in a division of a major multinational company, helping plan a two-day strategic planning conference. After we interviewed a representative sample of employees at all levels, several cultural themes emerged. Two in particular stood out: At the operations level, the products from various plants in the manufacturing division did not always work together; at the human level, relationships between the marketing division and two other divisions—research and development, and manufacturing—were very poor.

When we discussed these issues with the marketing managers who hired us, we were met with blank stares. We went up a notch, to a vice president who also did not seem to understand what we were talking about. With such denial, we knew we were on to something culturally significant, so I wrote a letter to the president, outlining the themes and saying we would call. The next week, I called Jack, the president, who said, "Thank you for calling. Your letter has been sitting on my desk. I did not think that anyone could see this problem. It is of great concern to me. When can we get-together?"

At our meeting, we said we would like to interview a broad sample of managers across Marketing, Manufacturing, R&D, and Customer Service, to understand what lay behind the issue. Jack gave us a free hand. After interviewing many managers at different levels in these divisions, several vice presidents, and three executive vice presidents, we met with the president and revealed our findings. The interviews showed why the issue seemed not to exist or was untouchable: because it came from the top of the company.

Something upper management did was encouraging the split. It was too dangerous for lower levels to talk about it. We were determined to unearth the secret.

At our meeting, we laid out the themes, asking Jack if there was anything he might be doing that signaled it was O.K. to not connect, not communicate. Jack rejected this idea immediately. "I have told each of my group presidents that they must improve communications and relationships between their divisions."

"And how did you tell them?"

"I called them into my office and told them."

"Did you do it as a group or individually?"

"Of course I did it with them individually. They are in England, Europe, the Far East, Australia, Latin America, Canada, and all across the U.S. We get-together as a group twice a year to discuss the financial plan. No, I talked to them when they were here individually on other business."

"And what do you think they did with your message?"

"We are very thorough. They know what to do. I am sure they met with each of their vice presidents and told them to get more coordination and cooperation."

"Do you think they did it one-on-one or as a group?"

"I am sure they called them in individually. Their people travel a lot and work in many different places. It is very difficult to get them all together at once."

"And do you think the message went down the line that way?"

"Yes, I am sure it did. We are very good at getting information down."

"Jack, do you see any connection between what you said and how you said it?"

"What do you mean?"

"Well, you told them individually to cooperate, to work together as a team."

"I just told you. It is very difficult to get them all together. I have to do it individually."

"I understand, but do you see that doing it individually is what we are talking about. What if you had got them together as a group and discussed teamwork and cooperation?"

"I just told you, we can't get-together for things like that."

Jack was becoming frustrated, even a little angry. We backed off, realizing we had hit on a corporate nerve. Here was Jack telling us that the issue was untouchable, just as the first vice president had told us by his blank, uncomprehending stare.

Over the next several months, we tried many routes but found no way to approach the issue. As the consultation progressed, it became clear that Jack saw the problem as a personality issue, that one of the group presidents, because of his "tank commander" style, was causing the split. Jack pulled out six years of evaluations on this manager, showing me that each year he'd asked him to correct the issue.

I thought, "What you do speaks so loudly I can't hear what you say." Here was the president, in full denial of the relationship between action and meaning on a theme that was so clear to me and (though untouchable) so clear to those below.

That is how organizational cultures work. When you unearth a big theme it may be unapproachable. You know the saying: "You can't get there from here!" Though people may complain, they get gratification from the work culture as it is. Almost everyone has some turf on which they can exert control over their own life, and over others. It feels good. Cultures hang together, make sense, are coherent. Everyone buys in. There is no another way.

❖ **Work cultures are very stable. Sometimes they would rather die than change.**

WHY THEY SHUT DOWN THE HAWTHORNE STUDIES

The now-famous Hawthorne studies illustrate two points:

▶ Control is more important than productivity.
▶ Little has changed in the last 70 years.

In 1927, at the Hawthorne plant of the Western Electric Company, the Mayo group from Harvard investigated the effect of changing light levels on telephone assemblers' productivity. The Mayo group assumed that raising light levels would increase production. It did. As a study control, they lowered the light levels, expecting that productivity would drop. It did not.

No matter how light levels changed, productivity rose, except when the light level was so low that the assemblers could not actually see the pieces.

It was not until 1939 that social scientists agreed on an interpretation of what happened. They announced what we now call the Hawthorne Effect, which says the obvious: "If you pay attention to people, they will respond." The researchers were looking at light levels and physiology. The assemblers experienced caring, receiving attention.

The truly culturally interesting part of the studies is not the Hawthorne Effect but the fact that although productivity at the plant increased steadily over three years, management stopped the experiment. After discussion with managers and many years of reflection, the researchers concluded that the company feared a loss of control over workers. The company culture—through management—traded away productivity for control.

IF YOU WERE TRULY INTERESTED IN PRODUCTIVITY, YOU WOULD NOT DO WHAT YOU ARE DOING

If productivity really interested a company, would it do what it does? Most managers spend over 30% of their time justifying what they do, responding to seemingly irrelevant requests from superiors, and dealing with unnecessary conflicts among people, departments, or with the union—unnecessary because these conflicts stem from poor relationships and mistrust (which can be overcome) that lead to miscommunications and misunderstandings.

If productivity really interested managers, would they allow these wasteful patterns to continue? They do, so I assume that others things are more important* and that people at all levels in the company get some satisfaction with things the way they are.

The Hawthorne studies were the first documented example of a work culture's resistance to productivity improvements. Western Electric executives feared a loss of control over workers.

My own experience with dozens of efforts to develop organizational cultures confirms that most work cultures are similar. Managers talk profitability and results, but their actions defeat them. If they wanted productivity, they would create a setting that engages people with the task. Their actions speak louder than their words.

Organizational cultures and managers are ambivalent about what they do. Managers know better ways, but they do not believe that the company culture would accept these.

❖ **Behavior reveals that the bottom line is not productivity. The real bottom line is conforming to the company culture.**

---

* A shortage of skill or knowledge is not the issue. Outside the organization's culture these managers breeze through similar situations with ease. Outside they know what to do and how to do it.

HOW SYSTEMS STOP CULTURE DEVELOPMENT EFFORTS

In large organizations, most culture development efforts begin with a nonconformist manager independent enough to step outside the mainstream. When that manager is promoted or retires, the new manager, conforming to the traditions of the work culture, usually tries to move the local culture backwards. From my own experience over 20 years, these four examples are typical:

► In a 15,000-person company, a plant manager, supported by an executive vice president, encouraged greater involvement at his 800-person plant, one of a dozen in the company. After three years, employee involvement was high, grievances were all but gone, productivity had climbed from about 60% of capacity to near and above the plant's engineering design limits.

Several years later the plant manager was promoted to vice president. The incoming plant manager, under a new senior vice president, did not understand or accept the open work culture. But the plant culture was solidly in place and his efforts to convert to an authoritarian management style met with great resistance. Frustrated, he left after 18 months and was replaced by a similar manager. By replacing department managers with more autocratic people, the new plant manager gradually increased fear and reduced openness.

► In a 50,000-employee company, an executive vice president supported an experiment with culture change at one unionized 1,000-person plant. He said, "I know it will take a long time. I don't want to hear from you for at least 18 months. Stay away from headquarters because they will want to measure results. If you don't show measurable change in six months, they will stop the work." Three years later, after managers and supervisors at the plant had learned to involve workers, grievances had fallen. Managers had time to focus on planning and production support, employees were more engaged, so productivity rose.

As part of a buyout, the executive vice president retired and a competitor hired away the plant manager. The replacement manager was "kick ass, take names." He and his lieutenants did not understand or want employee participation. The plant culture returned to the previous adversarial style. Resentment was high. Some employees set a major part of the plant on fire; it burned to the ground. Management chose to see the fire as unconnected to their authoritarianism.

► At a 20,000-person manufacturing company, a vice president supported culture change at a 250-person unit run by a courageous manager securely close to retirement. After two years, the significant improvements at this unit caught the attention of the manager's peers. These other unit managers also began involving employees. At the first unit, trust, openness, communications, and productivity rose, while costs dropped dramatically. The manager retired and his replacement was seen by many as "political." He brought in an autocratic assistant.

The management team and those below quickly sensed the danger. They no longer felt the same trust and support. They began to close down. Authoritarian behavior became more common. Meetings became dangerous. Most people were confident that the system would not revert completely because too many new participation processes were in place, too many people were on board with the new way. It was a most painful time.

► In a 25,000-person company, a unit vice president supported greater employee participation and more open communications within a 2,000-person unit. After three years, the management team became quite open. Supervisors responded by involving first line employees in decisions. Work related injuries and grievances dropped, while productivity increased steadily as relationships improved with the union leadership and with members. As union contract negotiation time neared, both union leaders and unit managers agreed that their improved relationships averted what would have been an almost certain strike over the wage reduction contract. During contract negotiations, the JLMC temporarily suspended meetings but agreed to maintain an informal and open line of communications, separate from the adversarial negotiations process controlled by the corporation's Industrial Relations department.

A change at the top of the company led to a new vice president (an accountant) questioning the return on investment of the employee involvement efforts. Although convinced that the improvements resulted from their efforts to change work culture, unit managers could not prove this. The accountant terminated the culture change activities. Managers and supervisors at the facility heard the message loud and clear: they no longer had support. While the work culture did not revert, managers and supervisors stopped expanding the involvement program.

For me, this last example was a textbook case showing that actions at higher levels of the culture (the human) are invisible from lower levels (the economic). Improved performance was facility-wide, not linked to anything specific and so not visible to an executive looking for narrow cause-effect relationships.

Although these cases are typical of how company cultures respond to culture change efforts, they should be seen in a broader context. American companies are struggling to break through to the next level. Evolution is not a smooth, rational path; stops and starts, backsliding, are all part of the process. In the long run, evolution is a one-way road. In the short run, it can falter.

Meanwhile people who have experienced the more developed, involving, open landscape know it is there. When the work culture regresses, they know all is not lost, just temporarily out of sight. Perhaps years will pass before it returns—but return it will.

WHY MANAGERS RESIST EMPLOYEE INVOLVEMENT*

This study is typical of the "people as objects" perspective that fits the arrested cultural view and much of sociology. Klein talks about people as objects, as input-output, action-reaction, or cause-effect devices. By focusing on individual behavior and not the situation, sociology reinforces existing work cultures, ignoring the fact that behavior reflects the work culture and the leadership and is almost always appropriate to the situation. Nevertheless, Klein makes some worthwhile points. Her research showed that most managers see employee involvement as good for the company. Less than half feel it is good for them, so they do not support the effort. Klein sees several reasons:

Lack of upper management commitment. Upper managers start the program but do not participate. The message is, "Give verbal support but no commitment."

No manager or supervisor participation. If work teams have only first line employees, then supervisors or managers do not know what is happening and cannot influence the group's work. This threatens their control and authority and they retaliate.

Exaggerated role reversal. From being typical directive leaders, the supervisors reverse their position, saying, "That's not my job, that's the team's problem." By taking a completely hands-off approach, they undermine the team.

Job security threatened. "If they solve their own problems, then what is my job?" Supervisors have difficulty juggling the facilitator role with their old directive role.

Extra work. The participation programs make more work for managers, which they must add to an already loaded day.

Rejection of concept. Some supervisors simply do not believe in the principles of employee involvement. They may have many reasons:

► They do not believe in participation and equality, or

► They fear losing prestige and their leadership role, or

► They doubt the sincerity of upper management. "The next level up doesn't really practice what they preach," or

---

*Adapted from Klein, Janice A. "Why Supervisors Resist Employee Involvement," *Harvard Business Review*, September-October 84, Number 5, pp. 87-95

- ▶ They feel that they are being left out of the program, or
- ▶ The program interferes with special one-on-one relationships with workers (favoritism).

So what can you do?

☞ You must be a role model. What your managers do reflects what you do. You might even ask supervisors what it would take to convince them of your commitment.

Start by paying attention to your own experience. What do you like from your boss, in discussions, in meetings? What you like is probably what others like. What can you do to give others that experience? For example:

- ▶ Involve supervisors in designing and carrying out the involvement effort. Instigate discussions about their own jobs.
- ▶ Delegate more real authority to supervisors so that they can properly respond to the participation process.
- ▶ Promote supervisor meetings or dinners—with no upper managers present—to encourage teamwork and discussion.
- ▶ Try to build a common language and philosophy about change.
- ▶ Involve supervisors in your own problems. Ask them for ideas. Share your performance review. Get their suggestions on how you can reach your goals.
- ▶ Look over the "21 ways to develop your organization's culture" on page 128. Pick one that you feel suits you and your work culture. Try it.

Remember this work culture development maxim: "If you know where you are going (a humane work culture), it does not matter where you start"—perhaps with your very next action.

❖ **If people resist change, it is because the work culture tells them to.**

TOUGH, HARD, ARRESTED WORK CULTURES

Many work cultures are tough, hard, unbalanced. They have yielded to authoritarianism and sit at an early developmental stage. Sometimes these work cultures are called "hyper-masculine," "boyish," or "arrested" in their development—blocked at some point on the natural path of maturing. They think and behave in simplistic ways. Here are some descriptions:

▶ Stressing analysis (pulling things apart) rather than synthesis (how things relate to each other).

▶ Separating thought from feeling, leadership from caring, thinking from action, work from pleasure. Putting science and technology ahead of human values and talking about people and human affairs using the kind of analysis and mechanistic science that underlies technology. Talking of people as objects rather than as subjects.

▶ Abstracting events or problems for analysis and then basing decisions on the abstract analysis as if it were real; for example, focusing only on the efficiency of a machine and then treating the operator as if she were simply an attachment to the machine.

▶ Focusing on a single purpose, making everything else instrumental to it; for example, changing equipment regardless of the operators' views or treating employees as "manpower," putting aside all concern for them as human beings.

▶ Engaging in grim, concentrated shop-talk at work, relieved only by weekends of pro football.

Your organization shows all these qualities to some degree. They are part of any mature work culture or person. In the arrested work culture, they are exaggerated. By opening the culture you will help it incorporate higher developmental levels (page 52). There your organization will stabilize for some time; then, if all goes well, it will step up once again.

FEAR AND RESISTANCE TO CHANGE

We have all experienced fear. The day after a major fire at a remote facility, a vice president said, "My boss wants to find out what really happened, and he wants some heads on the table. I can do one or the other. I can't do both." If people are afraid, they will not be open. If people feel safe, they will speak freely. People are afraid to do what they believe is not culturally acceptable. We learn early what groups can do. In my junior high school, I watched a physically frail Jewish boy suffer the taunts of classmates. I hated the taunting, but I did nothing. I was afraid. The book and film *Lord of the Flies* describes what groups do to a "strange" member. It is the same at work. Only fools go against the grain. Your career might stall; you could be fired, isolated, or sent to the dead pool. Sometimes a manager will sense encouragement from above, but later support fades. I have seen managers panic, caught at sea when calm waters suddenly got stormy.

Studies of "resistance" like the one on page 122 do not get close to describing a manager's real experience. **Upper managers might think that supervisors resist change. The reality is that the work culture does not support change.**

It is easy to look up, singling out a particularly harsh senior manager as culprit. Yet that senior manager is also doing what he or she believes is appropriate to the organization's culture. Do you go to the board, or do you consult the organization's history? Even if you could fully describe a company culture (which you cannot), it would be like a snake eating its tail. We make culture and it makes us; culture and people are inseparable.

Fortunately courage is also a human attribute. Sometimes a courageous manager will take his ship out in rough waters. As Bob, the mid-level manager described on page xi, said to me, "All my life I wanted to do this, to have a plant where people enjoyed their work." Bob was a brave manager who, by developing his own plant's culture, cut a new trail. The rest of his company followed.

❖ **If you manage by fear, you cannot have honesty.**

BEFORE YOU BEGIN, PREPARE

Developing a company culture is not necessarily smooth sailing. Here are a few experiences, recommendations, and warning flags from managers who have walked the path of work culture change for several years:

▶ At the start, try to envision the workplace you want. You might face strong resistance from your managers. If so, you cannot be "political" and go along with their objections or nothing will change. This is the lonely part of leading any company culture change. You must stand fast to your commitment.

▶ You need an honest objective understanding of your work culture's position at the beginning of the journey. This almost always necessitates an outside perspective. For some leaders, a consultant can be an impartial observer and ally in thinking about the way things are. The culture consultation requires the participation of the management team and begins the change process as it explores the existing culture through interviews.

▶ Understand that internal roadblocks will be placed in the path of change; those most threatened will create obstructions. If you are a unit in a large company, members of your management team, sensing you are straying from familiar waters, start worrying about how they will be seen by upper management, on whom their future careers depend.

▶ You will get a mixed reaction from the home office. On the one hand you will get more visits—people enjoy coming to a workplace where they feel welcomed and where people obviously enjoy what they are doing. On the other hand change is threatening. For example, as you push authority and control to lower levels you might hear, "I think you should get out there, they seem to have lost control. Managers have given away the store. They are not making decisions. They spend a lot of time just talking." There might be few supportive comments about your improved performance. In one case, the productivity improvement from the developing work culture was so dramatic, corporate managers actually sent out an audit team, suspecting the local manager might be juggling the books.

▶ From your peers (other unit managers), expect mixed reactions. On the one hand, people appreciate a trailblazer who takes on the dangers, marking a safe trail for them to follow. On the other hand as your unit's performance improves, people will begin requesting transfers to your unit. Your boss hints that perhaps your peers should try what you are doing. As problems in your unit disappear, and as your team does audacious things (new products, acquisitions, processes, etc.), your peers will be threatened, expressing this as hostility. As one manager who became the recipient of almost all company performance awards said, "It is a lot safer to run in the middle of the pack. Being this far out in front is dangerous. You can be easily picked off."

▶ As the work culture develops, suppliers and contractors will begin to say that it is different working with you. As people find ways to make things work better, solving system problems and improving the work processes, you will hear, "People are no longer blaming or looking for fault. They are finding ways to make it work. It is easier to get things done with you now."

21 WAYS TO DEVELOP YOUR ORGANIZATION'S CULTURE

Any of these might be a good place to begin testing the water:

1. Look in the mirror, page 7. As leader you hold the key.

2. Hold monthly "communications" meetings, page 65.

3. Interview, page 58.

4. Discuss interviews with your team. Look for themes, page 63.

5. Take your team on a "human half" retreat, page 70.

6. Use the four step decision process, page 80.

7. Use words from evolution levels 4 and 5, page 52.

8. Gradually put in place parts of a "parallel organization," page 64.

9. Try thinking field or process, not lineally or event, page 4.

10. Ask yourself are you sure that a humane, open work culture is really the most productive? page 17. Do your actions show that?

11. Watch for splits, page 12.

12. Try leading by asking questions, page 86.

13. Work on separating process from substance, page 74.

14. Make your own appraisal, down, sideways, and up, page 104.

15. Make your first thoughts of any problem begin with the upper half of the work culture; start with the people, page 11 and 52.

16. Involve those who will work with the new hires in the hiring process, page 103.

17. Involve those who will work with a newly promoted person in the selection and promotion process, page 102.

18. Make ranking and evaluation a group process, page 106.

19. Share your performance appraisal and goals with your subordinates, page 104.

20. Do not make management decisions in the corridor, or one-on-one, if the subject might affect someone not present. Use a formal decision process involving the affected people, page 80.

21. Think about yourself as a model of what you want the work culture to become. You and the unit's culture can walk the path together, page 135.

USING A CONSULTANT

It is very difficult for leaders to change a work culture purely from within. We are each captives of our company culture. Cultures blind us to other possibilities. Many senior managers use a mentor or friend outside their company to get a fresh perspective on operational issues. It is the same with culture change. It is almost essential to have the perspective and assistance of an outsider.

When working with an outsider on developing your organization's culture, do not ask for, or expect, reports. Reports, with their inevitable analysis, feed into the dominant pattern of companies; they emphasize the lower, operational half of the work culture. The consultant's time should be 95+% working with managers, individually and in groups, on regular actions and on interviewing.

How fast change occurs depends entirely on the culture's readiness. This readiness depends largely on the leadership. Some work cultures are very ready, others hesitant. You will usually see some changes in just a few months. In a system that is primed, you should expect that in two or three years, the overall organization's culture will take a big step up to a new level.

In a facility of 150-800 people, you might expect the consultant to be on-site between one-half and three days per week. Consultants work in teams of two of more people so they can understand and discuss cultural themes. Off-site time is minimal. The more people in the company, the more consultant time is needed. Small organizations, with fewer than 100 people, may find that two days a month is enough. Size and readiness set the pace.

Whatever the organization's size, the leader must expect to spend at least an hour every two weeks with the consultant, discussing themes, his or her own experiences and issues, and reflecting on the overall program. Because the top person's role and behavior is key to developing the work culture, these regular one-on-one discussions are critical. In large, complex, intense culture development efforts, these regular meetings may take several hours.

The full top management team must take at least two hours per month for the management communications meeting.

Culture change is hard work. As one manager said, "This is the hardest thing I have ever done, and I have started plants from scratch. But this is the most exciting and most important."

The pull of the company's culture on your managers is strong. When I started this work some 20 years ago, I consulted to a 3,000-person organization. After many interviews, I did not know whether the company was crazy or I was. Everyone said the same thing (in this case about clients and markets), but I could not believe it was realistic. I hired Royal Foote, one of my current partners, to consult with me. Our discussions revealed that what the organization was telling me about its markets was indeed unrealistic but was culturally supported. They almost had me convinced.

Together Royal and I helped the organization face its denial and get back on track. I learned my lesson: Culture consultants should always work as a team. Work cultures are simply too seductive.

Changing the work culture is not a program of the month. Do not blow the trumpets and run the flag up the pole. Do not hire trainers or packaged programs. That will all be seen for what it is, top-down business as usual. Begin with the management team and slowly build from there. Listen to your people. They will tell you what to do. Look for windows of opportunity and support them.

Good luck. Cultural leaders are heroes to their people. Most people want a better organizational life. They will respond quickly to your invitation.

Cultural development means personal development for employees and managers.

The Ideal—A Person–Centered Work Culture

S ome years ago, a manager said what he liked most about his plant's developed culture was its resilience. The corporation liked to try new product runs at his plant because the changes did not disrupt people and production as they did at other plants in the system. People relished the changes. They were proud that corporate managers viewed them so well. Change excited and challenged them. The work culture was well-developed.

As the work culture opens and managers become more flexible and responsive, employees become more flexible, more self-determining. As employees grow in their work roles, becoming more creative at solving their own work problems, they push on managers to grow and be more open. If managers continue to be open and responsive, this growth process continues.

As upper management opens the unit's culture to participation, the gift they receive in return is their own human development. Many managers report that developing their organization's culture has changed their own lives at work and at home.

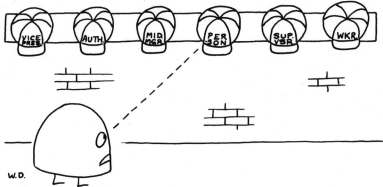

PEOPLE AT THE CENTER—THE AMERICAN WAY

There is no better guide to responsible life in organizations than America's traditional values of tolerance, freedom, truth, and unity amid diversity. The organization must see that employees cannot seek the truth unless they have freedom, that they will not care about freedom unless they have justice, and that justice depends upon a climate of care and trust. The only way to have unity in an organization is to have people at the center. What is good for people is good for the organization. Open, developed work cultures are very American.

In an ideal company culture, people enjoy coming to work, to the office, the lab, the plant, the shop floor, or the warehouse. There is no sharp distinction between work and pleasure because each person has room to fulfill him or herself through work.

Such organizations are productive beyond the limits assumed by most managers or the engineers who design the facility. Jack Welch, the CEO of General Electric says, "We believe there is an infinite capacity to improve."

As we learn to develop mature company cultures, the U.S. steps up the cultural ladder to a rung barely visible to the rest of the world. When I talk about such work cultures with managers from other countries, I feel that for them the idea of a humane open work culture, as we mean it, does not exist. As American companies explore the front edge of cultural evolution, the rest of the world is reaching for, or exploring, lower levels of democracy.

People in other countries might live their personal lives at mature levels outside their organizations, but in most countries— and still in most U.S. corporations—the corporate world limits the potential of its members, not seeing what our more adventurous corporate cultures are exploring.

❖ **Leadership's challenge is to develop and protect the humanness of everyone concerned by energetically pursuing the corporate purpose.**

MANAGER, KNOW THYSELF

For managers to rise into roles as cultural leaders they must experience at least three things:

► Be aware of themselves and what they do and the effect of what they do, of their philosophies, objectives, and styles of leadership on others.

► Feel supported and safe in trying alternative ways of attaining their objectives.

► Believe it is legitimate to be interested in employees and take satisfaction from working with people.

Of these goals, the first is the most basic. Many organizational cultures do not encourage managers to pay attention to or discuss their values, feelings, and experiences. The language of most companies includes little talk about humanness, about feeling, passion, needs, wants, drives, and experiences. To judge by most company conversations, you would think real people hardly existed or were just an expense, an instrument to achieve corporate goals. The truth is that corporate financial goals are easily achieved if people become the focus of activities.

If the manager can achieve this self-awareness at work, it will be easier to see employees as people. The more familiar the manager is with her own feelings and anxieties, as well as satisfactions, the greater her ability to understand what employees are thinking and feeling. She will become more conscious of her behavior and be better able to see her effects on others.

The human side of the workplace is not taught in management programs other than pseudo-science classes on "organization development." Nor will you find such discussions in popular management writings. It is as if real people, with real feelings, real passions, are not there. But they are.

Without encouragement from an outsider, leaders and managers find it very difficult to discuss these things at work.

THE GOLDEN RULE

We should behave toward others in such a way that if everyone behaved that way, we would all be better off. Adapted from Immanuel Kant —the categorical imperative, from: *Foundations of the Metaphysics of Morals*

Kant's words are a broader statement of the Golden Rule: "Do to others what you would like others to do to you." If people see that you are trying to lead with the right values, they are encouraged to follow suit. Most people want to do the right thing; they just never thought it was expected or valued. As leaders behave with more care, others follow, and the organization's culture steps up to a new level.

Conversely, when leaders are uncaring, everyone soon gets the message. Unfortunately, at higher levels in big corporations, managers are often too distant from outlying facilities. This distancing, together with the cultural inclination toward authoritarianism, leads them to treat operating units as only numbers and budgets.

In company after company, I see managers using energy to shield their people from this inhumane corporate context. The local managers know how disastrous such a context would be if it swept over the unit; morale would plummet and production falter.

❖ **It is right and good to have a broad view of our value and purpose in this world. Leading first with human values is good for people, good for those we love, and certainly good for the company.**

COMPETENCE AND SELF–DISCOVERY AT WORK

Until an employee experiences competence in some area, he or she is generally not ready to move on to the stage of self-discovery. After experiencing competence, a person will probably extend her interest into other areas, developing new and greater aspirations, thus expanding her personality.

As self-discovery grows, so does discovery of others. The maturing person uses her skills in genuine relationships with other people. She may find it enjoyable and appropriate to take a parental, or mentor, role with others in the organization.

Mary Lou, a production line worker, Teamster, and active participant in employee involvement teams at her plant, came to see herself as an active force in the company, a real problem solver and cultural leader. During an interview she said, "I didn't used to talk about what I did at home, at work. Now I talk about it all the time." Following this interview, in which Mary Lou also said, "I think women bring more of themselves to work than men," she went back to her production line and with the help of her fellow line workers set a new shift record.

Changing the quality of a person's work life is richly rewarding for leaders and followers. Creating settings where people can experience their competency and grow as human beings is part of a leader's role. In every situation described in this book I saw the people involved experience competency, mastery, greater self-control, and an expanded sense of who they are—at work.

This is the personal reward for leaders.

HUMAN RIGHTS AT WORK

Since its founding, the U.S. has actively explored and expanded the definition of human rights. Today this includes children's rights, women's rights, minority-ethnic rights, fetal rights, mother's rights—the list seems endless. It reaches into nonhuman areas, for example the rights of endangered species, the right of animals to be treated in humane ways, or the rights of the Amazon River ecosystem.

I attended an in-company training class on sexual harassment. Soon after the session began, a large welder in the back row stood up and said, "I don't want to talk about sexual harassment, I want to talk about harassment."

As companies build open organizations, they discuss and struggle with human rights and diversity in the workplace. The issue of civil rights at work, the right of employees to experience a productive, satisfying, and fulfilling workplace, is with us today. It may soon be in our courts.

"BOUNDARYLESS" ORGANIZATION

When a manager such as Jack Welch at General Electric uses the term *boundaryless company,* he means an organization that moves freely across national borders, while inside the company, information, ideas, and actions also move freely.

In systems terms, there is no such thing as a boundaryless organization. A system without a boundary is not a system. All systems maintain their integrity by controlling the flow in and out of resources, people, capital, information, and ideas. Boundaries are essential. How you manage them makes the difference.

Barriers are slowly dropping inside most American organizations. In 1978, a senior manager at Hewlett Packard told me that the heroes in upper management were those who had in their youth pushed an important business opportunity all the way to the top and back down to the right department and level. H-P was open to that behavior at a time when most corporations were not.

Today, as organizations emphasize teamwork and soften boundaries between levels and departments, traditional organization charts with military style lines of authority or command look more and more dated, a symbol of more autocratic times.

A manager recently showed me his new organization chart. It described the current state of his company, how things actually worked. There were no lines. He was on the bottom. First-line employees were on top. In between were people grouped in functional areas with the title of "coordinator." They were "support" to the first-line employees.

Such organization charts look strange. We are used to boxes and lines of authority, decision, and responsibility. But in an organizational culture where responsibility is pushed to the lowest level, where most decisions are participatory, where managers and supervisors provide support and give information about technical issues or customer needs, where people understand their roles and take personal authority and responsibility for their work, traditional charts showing lines of control have little connection to reality.

MANAGING CHANGE—CHAOS AT ONE LEVEL, ORDER AT ANOTHER

Every manager knows that the rate of change in society and the business world is accelerating. Defending against it is useless. Embracing change represents maturity in people and in work cultures.

Most people in organizations experience change as chaos because there is no stable base of relationships to stand on in the storm. If people experience chaos, they are telling us that the work culture is deficient.

If we trust the organization, if we have good relationships, if we are valued for our experience, if we are involved in decisions that affect us, if the workplace is a safe haven, then we will be secure, experiencing change as a natural part of our work.

☞ For leaders, the message is, if people are disturbed by change, then something is missing in the work culture. The missing piece is at the human level. As a first step, bring people together to share their experiences about changes. Write what they say on easel pads and pin these on the walls. Use change as an opportunity to build relationships, openness, and trust. Talk about your own concerns and experiences. Build on what happens.

❖ **In a developed work culture, change is not a threat—it is welcomed.**

THE INVISIBLE

It is only with the heart that one can see rightly; what is essential is invisible to the eye.
—Antoine de Saint-Exupéry, *The Little Prince*

The plant was an 800-person food processing operation, one of several in the corporation. After three years working on developing the plant culture, productivity made one of those sudden, predictable, evolutionary steps: it rose 40% over a three month period. Corporate headquarters sent out a team of engineers to analyze the plant's operations and report their findings.

The engineers stayed for a week, watching, asking questions, examining records, and measuring. Then they left to prepare their report. Gerry, the plant manager, commented, "They have no idea why this plant is so productive. The people here won't let it be unproductive. Those engineers can't see that it is everyone's attitudes that make it work so well. All they saw was what people were doing."

Some years later, after a spot-check audit from the National Sanitation Institute, the plant received a report saying it was "not only the cleanest plant in the corporation but the cleanest food processing plant in the United States." Again, why it was so clean was not visible; it had to do with values and attitudes. The sanitation crews were union members. Over several years, they had moved their jobs from low status, over-supervised positions to unsupervised, self-managed, high status crews. They put new members of the team on six months' probation, an unheard-of procedure in most union settings. The crews had their own areas, operating with the general understanding "Keep it clean." With full discretion and complete responsibility for a production area's cleanliness, every crew kept their area as spotless as if it were their own living room. The plant shone.

That is the real power of a developed work culture.

MANAGING COMPANY CULTURE—AMERICA'S SECRET WEAPON?

Other countries can barely see or understand what American organizations are beginning to explore at the cultural level. Even when offshore companies have participation efforts that look, on the outside, like our open work cultures, behind their actions is a meaning and human experience that is vastly different.

How can another country possibly compete with us after most of our companies have created engaging work cultures, open to what people have to give, when each person's full potential connects to the task?

The leverage of such a society is beyond our experience—so far.

SUMMARY OF SECTION THREE

► Work cultures are very stable.

► While talk in most organizations suggests productivity and profits are most important, behavior tells us that control is often more important.

► Efforts to develop a company culture are often resisted.

► Most organizational cultures are in a state of arrested development, behaving in simplistic ways.

► If people resist change it is because the work culture tells them to. In an engaging culture, change is welcomed.

► Human rights, the golden rule, participation, are all strong U.S. values. Developing the work culture is very American.

► How fast a culture develops depends on how ready it is to change. The stage for change is largely set by the leadership.

► Developing a work culture changes the lives of the leaders, at work and at home.

► What is essential in a mature culture is invisible to the eye. Attitudes, values, and meanings are not easily seen.

► How U.S. companies are developing their cultures is uniquely American and largely invisible to people from other countries.

REFERENCES

For the last 20 years the social sciences have increasingly tried to emulate the hard sciences. The result has been an emphasis on what can be measured, not always on what is important. Behaviorism is now ascendant; analysis, not synthesis, is dominant. Somewhere in this push for analysis the person was lost.

Companies are people doing things together, i.e. they are cultures. A book that ignores the person cannot be seriously discussing real organizations, leadership, or culture. Examine the index of the latest hot management book. Do the words "Person", "Personality", "Meaning", "Values", "Trust", or "Attitudes" appear? If not, be suspicious.

I have only included a few references. My comments are personal. Your reactions to these books and articles may be different.

Adorno, T.W., Frenkel-Brunswik, E., Levinson, D.J., and Sanford, R.N., *The Authoritarian Personality*, W.W. Norton & Company, Inc., New York, 1982. The definitive book on what continues to be the dominant issue in all societies and all organizations.

Argyris, Chris, "Good Communication That Blocks Learning." *Harvard Business Review,* July-August 1994, Vol. 72, Number 4. Argyris criticizes companies for not asking employees, "What goes on in this company that prevents you from questioning [poor] practices and getting them corrected or eliminated?". Good, real examples.

Bertalanffy, Ludwig von, *General System Theory*, George Braziller, New York, 1968. Still the very best systems book available. Read chapters 1, 2, 8, 9, & 10 for a brilliant overview of a usually difficult subject.

Boyle, Richard J., "Wrestling with jellyfish. An executive finds that becoming a participative manager is slippery business." *Harvard Business Review*, January-February 1984, Vol. 62, Number 1. Boyle's intimate, personal struggles with leading work culture change and its relationship to his family life. One of the best descriptions I know by an operating manager of leading a company's culture change.

Churchman, C. West, *The Systems Approach*, Delacorte Press, New York, 1968. A best seller in its day. Easy reading. A good summary of the more rational aspects of the field.

Collins, James, and Poras, Jerry, *Built to Last: Successful Habits of Visionary Companies,* HarperCollins Publishers, Inc., New York, 1994. This heavily researched book attempts to answer the question, "What makes truly exceptional companies different from other companies?" In the sociology-management genre, but worthwhile reading.

Colman, Arthur D., and Bexton, W. Harold, *Group Relations Reader 1*, (first published 1974). Selected writings based on work begun at the Tavistock Institute of Human Relations, London, England that promotes understanding of group and organizational processes that influence work, leadership, and authority. Also *Group Relations Reader 2*, edited by Arthur D. Colman and Mervin H. Geller, includes more recent interdisciplinary developments worldwide. Both are available from A.K. Rice Institute, PO Box 1776, Jupiter, FL 33468-1776, (408)-744-1350. (The A.K. Rice Institute also supports excellent experiential learning workshops throughout the US., on authority, leadership, and group relations.)

Doyle, Michael, and Strauss, David, *How to Make Meetings Work*. Berkley Publishing Group, New York, 1982. Simply the best and most comprehensive book on managing meetings but probably more than you really want to know.

Ghoshal, Sumantra, and Bartlett, Christopher A., "Changing the Role of Top Management: Beyond Strategy to Purpose", *Harvard Business Review*, November-December 1994, Volume 72, Number 6. Read with their following articles in HBR, Jan.-Feb. 1995, "Changing the Role of Top Management: Beyond Structure to Process", and HBR, May-June 1995 "Changing the Role of Top Management: Beyond Systems to People". The authors studied 20 large and vigorous European, US., and Japanese companies for 5 years. They find that successful leaders focus on Purpose, Process, and People. (If you would like a free two-page summary of these three excellent articles, send your business card with a note to Meridian Group, 1827A 5th Street, Berkeley, CA 94710, phone 1-800-363-7434, FAX 510-848-4257, or E-mail MeridianGr@AOL.com.).

Hall, E.T., *Beyond Culture*, Doubleday, New York, 1977. After Schein, a good book on organizational culture.

Keirsey, David, and Bates, Marilyn, *Please Understand Me, Character and Temperment Types*, Prometheus Nemesis Book Company, Del Mar, California, 1984. Are you an extrovert or introvert, thinker or feeler, or....? We each see the world in different ways. A Jungian psychologist's look at these differences.

Klien, Janice A., "Why Supervisors Resist Employee Involvement," *Harvard Business Review*, September-October 84, Number 5, pages 87-95. A sociological study of organizations that attempted increased employee involvement.

Lazlo, Ervin, *Evolution, The Grand Synthesis*, New Science Library, Shambala, Boston, 1987. Complex, integrative, the big picture of evolution.

Loevinger, J., and Wessler, R., *Measuring Ego Development*, Jossey-Bass, Inc., San Francisco, 1970. A detailed sociological description of the developmental process.

Mitchell, Russell, "Managing by Values: Is Levi Strauss' Approach Visionary—or Flaky?," *Business Week*, August 1, 1994, Number 3383. Chairman and CEO Robert Haas says of his company's values-based strategy, "We are doing this because we believe in the interconnection between liberating the talents of our people and business success." In this article *Business Week* expresses the current ambivalence in American companies to placing people first.

Sanford, Nevitt, *Learning After College*, Montaigne, Inc., Orinda, CA, 1980. An excellent overview of adult development. Sanford, the principal author of *The Authoritarian Personality*, discusses how it was before the hard sciences took over psychology. A good reminder of what adult living is about.

Schein, Edgar H., *Organizational Culture and Leadership*, San Francisco: Jossey-Bass, San Francisco, 1988. For me, the finest book on organizational culture, what it is, how to think about it.

INDEX

Organization chart, no lines, 138
Organizational cultures
 are unbalanced, 53
Organizations are like stacked
 families, 26

P

Pairing, in groups, 35
Parallel organization, 64
Parents, becoming your own, 25
Participation processes, 15
Passion, 133
Patton, General, 27
People
 as objects, 12, 124
 as subjects, 124
 flexible 80% your largest ally, 8
 to solve problems, use, 55
Person-centered work culture, 131
Personal agendas, 34
Personality, 5
 and culture, 19
 and decision making, 87
 development scale, 22
 limits cultural development, 29
 resonate to work culture, 87
Personality palette, 6
Philosophy, 48
Physics, first step of evolution, 46
Plus/Delta, meeting evaluation, 98
Poker, 70
Politics, 48
 group, 34
Postpone, response to hostility, 94
Power, 37
 of culture, 140
 over people, control, 37
 the ability to do work, 37
Powerful person, definition of, 37
Problems, to involve people, use, 55
Process, 9, 67, 80, 84
Processes for participation, 15
Production process, managing, 108
Productivity, 48, 140
 high comes easily, 17

large increases in, 29
 not the bottom line, 118
Profits, 48
Promoting, 102
Psychological safety, xiii

Q

Quality Circles, 19, 67
Questions to lead by, 86

R

Ranking managers for pay raises
 and bonuses, 106
Relationships, 15, 49
Resilience, xiii, 131
Resistance to change, 125
Responding to hostile questions, 94
Retreat, 70
Richelieu, E.L., 49
Rocks, 9
Role, 122, 136
 in EIT unusual for managers, 67
 in interview, 60
 models, leaders as, 15
Roots of Western culture, 9

S

Sartre, J.P., 7
Scylla, 9
Secret voting, 91
Self-awareness, 10, 50
Self-consciousness, 50
Self-control, 37, 38
Sexual harassment, 62, 137
Shakespeare, W., 6, 36
Silence
 use to manage group, 92
Situation, 5
Sociology, 48
Splits, 12
Stage, culture is the, 6
Strong leaders, 15
Substance, 80
Superstructure, 9
Supportive environment, 4

TO PURCHASE THIS BOOK

Please shop at your local bookstore. Your bookstore can order this book through Independent Publishers Group (IPG), Chicago. To order call 1-800-888-4741. Visa and Master card accepted.

CORPORATE VOLUME DISCOUNTS

To place a corporate order for 10 or more copies of this book, phone 1-800-363-7434 (Fax 1-510-848-4257) for volume discounts and shipping.

Context Press
1827A 5th Street
Berkeley, CA 94710

Same day shipping. Please have your Purchase Order number ready.

Barry Phegan, Ph.D., President of Meridian Group, Berkeley, has 25 years experience helping companies build more productive and satisfying workplaces where shared values support business goals. For 15 years before that he was an employee and manager in the US, Canada, Sweden, and Australia. His Ph.D. is from the University of California, Berkeley, where he regularly teaches management classes.

TALK WITH THE AUTHOR?

Since 1976 Barry Phegan and Meridian Group have helped companies achieve their highest potential by improving:

- ► **Company culture**
- ► **Relationships and communications**
- ► **Morale, involvement and motivation**

They have helped management develop culturally sound processes for:

- ► **Attracting and keeping talented employees**
- ► **Managing rapid growth and change**
- ► **Managing the cultural integration process during mergers and acquisitions**

Barry Phegan is available for presentations in your company, or as a speaker at off-site meetings. For more information contact:

Meridian Group—Company Consultants since 1976
"Changing The Way People Work Together"
1827A 5th Street, Berkeley, CA 94710
Phone: 800-363-7434, 510-848-4258 | FAX: 510-848-4257
http://www. meridiangrp.net | email: dialogue@meridiangrp.net